INSIGHT GUIDES

Great Breaks

OXFORD

APA PUBLICATIONS **L**

Part of the Langenscheidt Publishing Group

Contents

Oxford's Top 10

From punting on the River Thames to grandiose historical colleges and the oldest botanic garden in Britain, here are at a glance the top sights and activities of this fascinating city

▲ **Magdalen College** (p.61). Dominating the eastern end of the High Street, Magdalen has a tower, cloisters, quads galore, even a deer park.

▲ **Punting on the Thames** (p.44). View the spires of Oxford from a punt on the river while sipping champagne and tucking into a picnic.

▲ **Ashmolean Museum** (p.86). The oldest museum in the country has a superb collection of art and antiquities.

▶ **Bodleian Library** (p.16). The library complex holds the circular Radcliffe Camera and the Divinity School.

▲ **Sheldonian Theatre** (*p.16*). Designed by Sir Christopher Wren, the Sheldonian – which seats up to 2,000 people – is used for university ceremonies, lectures and concerts.

▼ **Port Meadow** (*p.104*). Adjacent to the River Thames, this extensive flood plain is a great place to take time out from city sightseeing. The nearby Perch Inn is a popular stopping point.

▼ **Christ Church** (*p.69*). Oxford's largest college is home to the city's cathedral. Its dining hall was used as a location for scenes in the *Harry Potter* films.

▲ **University Museum** (*p.99*). A fine natural history museum, complete with dinosaur skeletons, is located in a Gothic pile next to Keble College.

▼ **Botanic Garden** (*p.52*). The oldest botanic garden in Britain, featured in Philip Pullman's *His Dark Materials* trilogy, contains a wealth of floral treasures and a steamy hothouse.

▲ **Covered Market** (*p.40*). This indoor market shelters traditional butchers, unique shops and cafés.

A Tale of Two Cities

Although Oxford owes its world-wide fame to its string of colleges, the 'city of dreaming spires' is really a tale of two cities – of town and gown

Oxford lies approximately 50 miles (80km) northwest of London. The core of the city occupies a gravel terrace between the upper River Thames (known in Oxford as the Isis) and the smaller River Cherwell (pro-

nounced 'Charwell'). The first major settlement was established here in Saxon times, probably on present-day St Aldate's, and the original 'oxen ford' from which the town gets its name is thought to have been where Folly Bridge stands today.

THE UNIVERSITY

The very first centres of learning in Oxford were monasteries established by the Augustinians in the early 12th century. But, as was the case elsewhere in Europe, the need arose for higher training than the local ecclesiastical schools could provide. In 1167, during a feud between Henry II and the King of France, the University of Paris was closed to scholars and they came and settled in Oxford.

In the 13th century, friars from the most prominent religious orders came into the town to teach, living and studying in large town houses or 'academic halls'. In the second half of the 13th century, rich, powerful bishops established their own centres of scholarship in the town, and the first colleges were born.

Today, the university comprises 38 colleges (eight for graduates only and one, All Souls, exclusively for Fellows – senior academic members), and almost 20,000 students. While the appeal of the city is the medieval atmosphere of many of its college quadrangles, much has changed since the early days. In the 19th century, under the inspiration of men such as John Ruskin, the university was reformed from being a medieval, clerical institution based on privilege to a modern educational establishment devoted to teaching and scholarship. But the colleges remain, as they always were, autonomous corporations with their own statutes.

Above: the stunning Radcliffe Camera graces the Oxford skyline.
Below: a cyclist's city.

Above: antique engraving depicting Oxford, with two scholars on the right (1575).

TOWN AND GOWN

The arrival of students in Oxford created friction with townspeople. Back in 1209 a local woman was killed by a scholar, and two of his unfortunate colleagues were hanged in revenge. The university went on strike and students fled in fear; some went to Cambridge where they founded Oxford's 'sister' university.

The problem was not just one of envy. As the colleges expanded, they took over land occupied by the townsfolk and their businesses, filling the city centre with seats of learning. This led to large-scale poverty, a problem compounded by the migration of the cloth industry to rural areas, and by the Black Death in 1349, which wiped out one-third of Oxford's population.

Matters came to a head on St Scholastica's Day in 1355, when a brawl between scholars and the landlord of the Swindlestock Tavern at Carfax escalated into a riot. For three days academic halls were attacked by townsmen supported by a mob of thugs brought in from the countryside. Dozens of scholars died. But the town paid the ultimate price by losing all its rights and privileges, and until these were reinstated by legislation in the 19th century, its fortunes were almost entirely dictated by the university. Some resentment continues to this day, partly as a result of the university's seeming reluctance to share its land and facilities with the town.

ECONOMY AND INDUSTRY

The canal arrived in 1790, and the railway in 1844, but the town, hampered by the overriding presence of the university, did not become part of mainstream industrial Britain until the early 20th century.

Above: relaxing on the quad at Corpus Christi College.

Ⓕ Proud Traditions

One of the most famous university traditions is June's Encaenia honorary degree ceremony. The Chancellor of the University leads dignitaries and dons along Broad Street and into the Old Schools Quadrangle before conferring the degrees at the Sheldonian. The scarlet-and-pink robes they wear are a reminder of the days before the Reformation when all university members were in holy orders. This applied to students, too, and their successors today still wear black-and-white 'subfusc' garments for exams and degrees ceremonies.

Above: during Encaenia, university dignitaries process to the Sheldonian Theatre in their colourful robes.

William Morris (later Lord Nuffield) started his bicycle business in the High Street in 1893. In 1912 he progressed to designing cars, and within a year opened his first factory out at Cowley. Morris Motors was born, and Oxford was transformed into an industrial centre. The apogee of car production at Cowley came in the 1970s. A long period of decline then followed, until the German car maker BMW started assembling the New Mini at the revamped Plant Oxford. The Mini, which is exported to over 100 countries, has been a runaway success.

But the university continues to exert a huge influence on the economic life of the city. Its long traditions in scientific research have put Oxford at the leading edge in the development of medical and industrial technology. Printing and publishing – industries that are almost as old as the university itself, with the first book printed in Oxford in 1478 – still thrive in the city, spearheaded by the Oxford University press, Blackwell's and Pearson Education. And tourism, the city's biggest industry after that of education, is booming despite the current global economic downturn.

Of course, with 3.5 million tourists a year, and up to 30,000 students during term-time (including those at Oxford Brookes, the city's other university), Oxford, with its permanent population of just 120,000, is constantly under pressure from development and congestion. However, around 52 percent of the city area is protected open space, including the great expanses of Port Meadow and Christ Church Meadow by the River Thames, University Parks and the banks of the Cherwell, as well as South Park rising to the east of the centre. Together with the verdant college gardens they provide wonderful oases for residents and visitors alike.

Guide to Coloured Boxes

Ⓔ Eating	This guide is dotted with coloured boxes providing additional practical and cultural information to make the most of your visit. Here is a guide to the coding system.
Ⓕ Fact	
Ⓖ Green	
Ⓚ Kids	
Ⓢ Shopping	
Ⓥ View	

Food and Drink

Intimate cafés, historic pubs and a Michelin-starred restaurant await the hungry and thirsty in Oxford.

As far as dining out is concerned, the cosmopolitan flavour of Oxford is reflected in the wide choice of cuisine offered by restaurants in the city and beyond. An influential figure in putting this provincial English city on the international culinary map in the late 20th century was the renowned chef Raymond Blanc, with his two Michelin-starred Le Manoir aux Quat'Saisons at Great Milton just outside Oxford, and his Brasserie Blanc on Walton Street in the lively district of Jericho (see p.107).

Nowadays, the city is served by the usual chains as well as some good independent restaurants, from the Lebanese Al Shami (see p.95) and the Thai Chiang Mai (see p.65) to the traditional British Gee's Restaurant (see p.103) and the Italian Luna Caprese (see p.103).

There's also a good range of restaurants with vegetarian and organic options, from the Nosebag on St Michael's Street (see p.83), an old favourite serving up large portions of hearty wholesome cooking, to more recent additions such as The Garden, at The Gardener's Arms pub, on Plantation Road in Jericho.

CAFÉS

Although the city is not associated with any particular special dish or food type – Frank Cooper's Oxford marmalade (see p.61) excepted, of course – it is blessed with a large number of appealing cafés, adept at serving thirsty students and visiting tourists in need of a break from sightseeing.

Long-standing student haunts include the beatnik Georgina's (upstairs

Above: Oxford is filled with delightful old pubs.

on Avenue 3 in the Covered Market, see p.43) and the traditional Queen's Lane Coffee House (see p.33), on the High Street. For a chic option try the gilded Grand Café (see p.65) – located, according to Samuel Pepys, on the site of the first coffee house in England – at the eastern end of the High Street; for a classic 'greasy spoon' there's none better than the St Giles' Café, a reliable establishment on the road of the same name. And for special occasions, such as graduations, a traditional choice is afternoon tea at the Randolph Hotel.

PUBS

For something traditional but rather more potent, Oxford also has more than its fair share of atmospheric old pubs. The most historic drinking holes in the city centre include the Eagle and Child on St Giles', a literary landmark, where writers such as C.S. Lewis and J.R.R. Tolkien once drank in the company of the Inklings literary group *(see p.95)*, the Lamb & Flag *(see p.103)*, also on St Giles, and the Georgian King's Arms *(see p.33)*, diagonally opposite the Sheldonian. Other historic pubs are the Turf Tavern *(see p.33)*, hidden down an alley by the Bridge of Sighs, The Bear *(see p.53)*, an intimate wood-panelled place near Oriel Square, and the tiny White Horse, on Broad Street.

Venture slightly out of the city centre, and the choice of good pubs extends further to include the Rose and Crown on North Parade in North Oxford, the The Anchor on Hayfield Road (north of Jericho near Port Meadow; also great food) and the Rusty Bicycle in Cowley. Further out still you get to the 17th-century Trout *(see p.107*, a regular feature on Inspector Morse) on the Thames at Godstow; highlights here include hearty food and peacocks in the garden. Still retaining its pub atmosphere, though serving decent meals as well, is The Plough at Wolvercote; a visit here can be combined with a pleasant walk along the adjacent canal.

FOOD SHOPPING

If you're looking for excellent-value produce, particularly butchery, pay a visit to the Covered Market, established in 1774. Foodies are well served here, particularly by several old-fashioned and outstanding purveyors of meats (originally the only foodstuff permitted to be sold in the market), but also by fine greengrocers, a cheesemonger and a fishmonger. There are also a number of independent cafés and the ever-popular cookie stall, Ben's, where irresistible treats are baked on the premises.

Oxford is also well supplied with shops selling alcoholic drinks. Among the most unusual are the Whisky Shop (www.whiskyshop.com) at No. 7 Turl Street and the Grog Shop (which specialises in unusual beers) at No. 13 Kingston Road, just beyond the end of Walton Street.

Find our recommended restaurants at the end of each Tour. Below is a Price Guide to help you make your choice.

Eating Out Price Guide

Two-course meal for one person, including a glass of wine.

£££	over £25
££	£15–25
£	under £15

Ⓕ The Brewing Tradition

Oxford has a long history of beer-making, with the first brewery established by the monks of Osney Abbey in the Middle Ages. Later, the colleges also brewed their own beer, with stiff competition between them to produce the strongest and tastiest ale. In the 1800s there were 14 breweries by the Castle Mill Stream and the canal. Today, there are no major breweries left in Oxford, the last one, Morrells, having closed in 1999.

Above: Morrells, founded in 1782, was Oxford's last brewery to close.

The Heart of the University

Follow in the footsteps of Harry Potter, Inspector Morse, Christopher Wren and Thomas Cranmer for an hour or two on this ¼ mile (0.4km) stroll around the university

While the busy crossroads of Carfax is usually considered the centre of the City of Oxford (see p.41), the university – founded as it is on the college system – has no such focal point. Yet there is one area that, by virtue of the historic role of its buildings, can be described as the heart of the university. Lying between the High Street and Broad Street, it also represents one of the finest architectural ensembles in Europe.

BEARDED ONES

At the eastern end of Broad Street, visitors are met by the intimidating gaze of the Emperors' Heads, or 'Bearded Ones', which tower over the railings separating the street from the precinct of the Sheldonian Theatre. Such

Highlights

- Emperors' Heads
- Museum of the History of Science
- Sheldonian Theatre
- Bodleian Library
- View from the spire of the Church of St Mary the Virgin

busts were used in antiquity to mark boundaries, but no one knows whom these particular ones represent. They were installed in 1669, the same year that the theatre was completed, but over the years their features eroded so considerably that they were no longer recognisable even as faces. Facelifts were performed by a local sculptor in 1970.

Preceding Pages: All Souls' College. **Left**: Bodleian Library. **Above**: one of the curious Emperors' Heads.

SCIENCE MUSEUM

To the right is the Old Ashmolean Museum, the original home of the famous art and antiquities museum before it moved to Beaumont Street *(see p.86)*. Designed by Thomas Wood and completed in 1683, it is considered one of the most architecturally distinguished 17th-century buildings in Oxford.

It now contains the **Museum of the History of Science ❶** (tel: 01865 277 280; www.mhs.ox.ac.uk; Tue–Fri noon–5pm, Sat 10am–5pm, Sun 2–5pm; free), with the world's finest collection of European and Islamic astrolabes, as well as quadrants, sundials, mathematical instruments, microscopes, clocks and, in the basement, physical and chemical apparatus, including that used by Oxford scientists in World War II to prepare penicillin for large-scale production. Also on display in the basement is a blackboard used by Albert Einstein in the second of his three Rhodes Memorial Lectures on the Theory of Relativity, which he delivered at Rhodes House, Oxford, on 16 May 1931. Part of the basement was once used as a dissecting room,

and set into the stone floor you can see a number of small holes. The legs of the dissection table were slotted into these holes to keep the table still while professors and students worked on the corpses. The museum also runs a programme of talks, guided tours and workshops. See the website for details of family events where you can look through old telescopes or take part in scientific experiments.

ORIGINAL UNIVERSITY PRESS

The imposing neoclassical edifice to the left of the heads is Nicholas Hawksmoor's **Clarendon Building**, erected in 1715 – erstwhile home of Oxford University Press. The OUP's first home was the basement of the Sheldonian Theatre, but this was far from ideal as compositors had to move out every time the theatre was required for a ceremony. However, between 1702 and 1704 the Press published its first bestseller, Lord Clarendon's History of the Great Rebellion, and subsequent profits enabled the University to erect this new building. The Press moved out of the Clarendon to its present site on

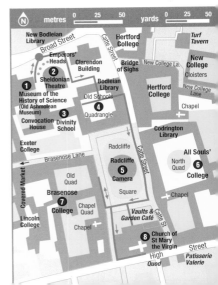

Walton Street *(see p.92)* in 1830, but it is still used for meetings of the Delegates of the Press, the University committee that directs its affairs. Around the roofline are James Thornhill's sculptures of the nine Muses.

SHELDONIAN THEATRE

Through the gateway is the **Sheldonian Theatre ❷** (tel: 01865 277 299; www.sheldon.ox.ac.uk; Mon–Sat 10am–12.30pm, Mar–Oct 2–4.30pm, Nov–Feb 2–3.30pm, though times can vary depending on functions; charge). Commissioned by Gilbert Sheldon, Chancellor of the University, in 1662, this was Christopher Wren's first architectural scheme, which he designed at the age of 30, while still a professor of astronomy. Modelled on the ancient open-air Theatre of Marcellus in Rome, but roofed over to take account of the English weather, the Sheldonian was built primarily as an assembly hall for more or less elaborate university ceremonies. Chief among these is the Encaenia – the bestowing of honorary degrees that takes place each June.

For most of the year, however, the Sheldonian is used for concerts *(see box below)*. It is not the most comfortable of venues, with its hard seats, but is a fine interior nonetheless, spanned

Above: The Sheldonian Theatre offers fine views from the rooftop cupola.

by a 70ft (21m) diameter flat ceiling, painted with a depiction of the *Triumph of Religion, Arts and Science over Envy, Hate and Malice*. The ceiling, with no intermediate supports, is held up by huge wooden trusses in the roof, details of which can be seen on the climb up to the cupola, which, though glassed in, provides fine views over central Oxford.

BODLEIAN LIBRARY

To the south of the Sheldonian, through the small gateway into Old Schools Quadrangle, are the buildings of the **Bodleian Library** (tel: 01865 277162; www.bodley.ox.ac.uk). Before admiring the beautiful main courtyard in too much detail, first journey back in time by entering the doors behind the bronze statue of the Earl of Pembroke (a university chancellor) and proceeding through the vestibule into the much older **Divinity School ❸** (tel: 01865 277 224; Divinity School only: Mon–Fri 9am–5pm, Sat 9am–4.30pm, Sun 11am–5pm; charge, except for children under 15). It is well worth taking a guided tour, since it will allow you to see areas not otherwise accessible, in-

---

F Music to the Ears

Ever since 1733, when Handel was honoured with a Doctor's degree in music, which was celebrated with a week of performances of his music here, the Sheldonian has been the venue for a large variety of classical concerts. For further information, contact Music at Oxford (www.music atoxford.com) or the Oxford Philomusica Orchestra (www.oxfordphil. com), which often performs here as well as at other venues in the city.

Harry Potter

The makers of the Harry Potter films made extensive use of Oxford as settings for numerous scenes. Most notably, the Divinity School became Hogwarts Sanatorium and Duke Humfrey's Library doubled up as Hogwarts Library. Other films set in various parts of the Bodleian complex include Philip Pullman's *The Golden Compass*, *Shadowlands* (about C.S. Lewis, author of *The Lion, the Witch and the Wardrobe*) and *The Madness of King George* (in which the Divinity School stands in for Parliament's House of Commons).

Above: Christ Church Hall *(see p.72)* also features in the *Harry Potter* films.

cluding Duke Humfrey's Library (tours Mon–Sat 10.30am, 11.30am, 1pm and 2pm, Sun 11.30pm, 2pm and 3pm, university ceremonies permitting; charge). The Bodleian runs a Family Tour and a History Trail for children.

Regarded by many as the finest interior in Oxford, work began on the Divinity School itself in 1426, follow-

Above: Divinity School vault.

ing an appeal for funds by the university. Being the most important of all subjects at the time, theology required a suitable space, but money kept running out and the room took almost 60 years to complete. Its crowning glory is the lierne-vaulted ceiling, which was added in 1478, after the university received a gift from Thomas Kemp, Bishop of London. Completed by local mason William Orchard, the ceiling is adorned with sculpted figures and 455 carved bosses, many bearing the arms of benefactors.

Candidates for degrees of Bachelor and Doctor of Divinity were not the only people to demonstrate their dialectical skill under this glorious ceiling. It was here, too, that Latimer, Ridley and Cranmer were cross-examined by the Papal Commissioner in 1554, then condemned as Protestant heretics *(see p.22 and 35)*.

DUKE HUMFREY'S LIBRARY

In around 1440, a substantial collection of manuscripts was donated to the university by Humfrey, Duke of Gloucester, the younger brother of Henry V. The walls of the Divinity School were built up to create a second storey for

Above: postcard-perfect – the Radcliffe Camera, the earliest example in England of a circular library, and All Souls' College to the right.

Duke Humfrey's Library (accessible only by guided tour – see *details above*). The library, with its magnificent beamed ceiling, was first opened to readers in 1488, but was defunct by 1550, largely as a result of neglect and the emergence of book printing (which rendered manuscripts redundant), but also owing to the depredations of the King's Commissioners after the dissolution. It was while he was a student at Magdalen College that Thomas Bodley became aware of this appalling state of affairs. Posted abroad as Ambassador to the Netherlands by Queen Elizabeth I, he used his far-reaching network of contacts to establish a new collection of some 2,000 books to restart the library. The room was restored and opened once more in 1602, and subsequently extended by the addition of the Arts End. Here, visitors can see original leather-bound books dating from the 17th century, some of them turned spine inwards so that chaining them to the shelves (a common practice) would cause less damage.

Old Schools Quadrangle

In 1610, an agreement was made whereby the library would receive a copy of every single book registered at Stationers' Hall. Soon, Bodley's collection had grown so large that a major extension was required, hence the **Old Schools Quadrangle** ❹. Though

Above: the view from Broad Street through the historic corridors of the Bodleian Library.

The quadrangle was also built as the new home of the various schools of the university. Their Latin names can be seen in gold lettering painted on a blue background above the doors. Above these is the library space, but the continuity around the quad is broken at the east end by the splendid gate-tower, or 'Tower of the Five Orders' – so named because it is ornamented with columns and capitals designed to provide students with an introduction to the five orders of classical architecture: Doric, Tuscan, Ionic, Corinthian and Composite. In a niche on the fourth storey is a statue of James I, the reigning monarch when the quadrangle was built.

RADCLIFFE CAMERA

Leaving the quad through the eastern exit and turning right, you come to the broad expanse of Radcliffe Square, dominated by the most familiar symbol of Oxford, the **Radcliffe Camera ❺** (closed to the public). Dr John Radcliffe, a famous Oxford physician, bequeathed the sum of £40,000 to found a library on his death in 1714.

only the cornerstone was laid before Bodley's death in 1613, this magnificent piece of architecture, designed in Jacobean-Gothic style, can be regarded as the culmination of his life's work. The quadrangle boasts a wonderful serenity, and despite being built much higher than college quads is still light and airy.

Ⓕ Underground Storage

The Radcliffe Camera is by no means the latest addition to the library. In 1930, the huge New Bodleian Library was opened on the other side of Broad Street to house the overspill. The new library is linked to the old one by a system of underground conveyors, and books lie just below the surface of Radcliffe Square. The Bodleian not only has to cope with a constant flow of new book titles, but also every single newspaper and magazine published in the UK – literally millions of items, including some priceless treasures. The New Bodleian is currently being revamped to make it more accessible to the public (completion 2015).

Above: there is certainly no shortage of books in Oxford.

Based on an idea by Nicholas Hawksmoor, this purely classical, circular building, surmounted by a dome, was ultimately designed by James Gibbs and completed in 1749. Absorbed as a reading room of the Bodleian in 1860, the building was part of a grand 18th-century scheme to open up this area of the city as a public square, and replace the existing jumble of medieval houses. Not all the plan was realised, but it is impressive how the circular Radcliffe Camera appears to fit so naturally into the rectangular square.

ALL SOULS'

To the east of the Radcliffe Camera is the gateway to the North Quadrangle of **All Souls' College** ❻ (visitor entrance on the High Street; tel: 01865 279 379; www.all-souls.ox.ac.uk; Mon–Fri 2–4pm; free). Founded in 1438, this is the only college in Oxford never to admit any students, restricting membership to Fellows only, providing them with facilities to pursue their research (as well as fine vintages from Oxford's largest wine cellar).

Much of the North Quad is the result of 18th-century alterations and additions, which came about after the medieval cloisters were levelled and a Fellow, Christopher Codrington – whose fortune was founded on the slave trade – bequeathed much of his estate, including a large collection of books, to the college. The resulting Codrington Library (viewing only by special permission) occupies the building on the north side of the quad. Designed by Nicholas Hawksmoor, the exterior (with the enormous sundial by Wren) is in Gothic style to mirror the chapel opposite, while the interior is purely Renaissance.

The eastern edge of the quad is dominated by distinctive twin towers, also by Hawksmoor, while the southern side accommodates the 15th-century chapel, complete with original hammerbeam roof and a magnificent reredos behind the main altar.

BRASENOSE COLLEGE

On the other side of Radcliffe Square is the main entrance to **Brasenose College** ❼ (tel: 01865 277 830; www.bnc.ox.ac.uk; generally open in the afternoons – telephone for exact times; charge). The battlemented gate-tower and the Old Quad behind it date from 1516, but the latter was altered a century later by the addition of attic rooms with dormer windows. The most distinctive feature of the quad is the sundial on the north wall. Looking back after crossing to the far side, visitors are treated to one of the most startling views in Oxford, with the huge dome of the Radcliffe Camera looming above the entrance tower, and the spire of St Mary's church to the right.

Brasnose College is named after the 'brazen nose' – a bronze door-knocker – that once hung on its gates.

Above: the disctinctive twin towers of All Souls' College.

Above: statue adorning the facade of the Church of St Mary the Virgin.

In medieval times, anyone fleeing the law could claim sanctuary within by grasping the knocker. However, in the 1330s some students stole the ring and took it to Stamford where they intended to establish a rival university. Edward II refused to sanction the breakaway institution, but the brazen nose remained on a house in Stamford until 1890, when the college bought the whole building in order to retrieve the knocker. It is now hung in the dining hall. Meanwhile, in 1509, a replacement knocker had been commissioned. Shaped like a human head, this can be seen at the apex of the college's main gate.

Immediately to the north of Brasenose, the narrow Brasenose Lane leads through to Turl Street and the Covered Market (see p.40). The cobbled gully down the middle marks the line of the original open sewer.

CHURCH OF ST MARY THE VIRGIN

The **Church of St Mary the Virgin** ❽ (tel: 01865 279 113; www.university-church.ox.ac.uk; daily 9am–5pm, July–Aug to 6pm; charge for tower), with its soaring 13th-century spire, completes the harmony of Radcliffe Square. It can be regarded as the original hub of the

Ⓥ Landmarks from the Tower

The views from the top of the University Church are superb. Due north is the Radcliffe Camera with the Bodleian Library behind. To the east, the High Street curves away towards the River Cherwell, with the bell-tower of Magdalen College in the distance. Due south, the squat tower in front of Christ Church Meadow is Merton College Chapel, while to the southwest looms the cupola of Christ Church's Tom Tower. At the top of the High Street to the west is Carfax with its tower, and beyond it the round, green spire of Nuffield College. Just below, is Brasenose College and, beyond, the neo-Gothic chapel of Exeter College.

Above: view of the High Street from St Mary's tower.

Above: St Mary the Virgin from the High Street side.

The Interior

Now entering the vestibule from the north side, visitors are first given the option to climb the tower (Mon–Sat 9am–5pm, Sun 11.45am–5pm; charge). After a series of steps and walkways, the ascent culminates in a narrow spiral staircase, which finishes at the gangway at the base of the spire.

Back down on the ground again, the 15th-century nave is a fine example of the Perpendicular Gothic style, with slender, widely spaced columns and large windows. Look out for the pillar opposite the pulpit in the north side of the nave which has been cut away; this was done to build a platform for the trial of Thomas Cranmer, Archbishop of Canterbury, in 1556, a major event in English history.

Cranmer faced his persecutors for the last time here. Having witnessed the deaths of fellow martyrs Bishops Latimer and Ridley six months earlier, he was already a condemned man. But the Papal Commissioner now expected him to denounce the Reformation. Cranmer refused to do so, instead retracting all the written recantations he had previously penned; he was dragged from the church and

university, for it was here in the 13th century that the first university meetings and ceremonies were held, and all the administrative documents kept.

Before entering via its north door you will see, on the left, the entrance to the Vaults and Garden Café *(see Eating Out, opposite)*. There can be few cafés with a history such as this, for it occupies the space of the former Convocation House, an annexe built in 1320 specifically to house the University governing body, which continued to meet here until 1534 when the administration moved to Convocation House at the west end of the Divinity School. The vault is beautiful, but in summer the garden is the perfect place to rest a while.

Above: church detail.

taken back to his cell in the Bocardo prison above the city's North Gate before being burned at the stake in Broad Street.

Oxford Movement

Almost 300 years later, the church was again the centre of controversy when, in 1833, John Keble preached his famous sermon on national apostasy. This led to the founding of the Oxford Movement, which espoused a renewal of Roman Catholic thought within the Anglican Church and whose ideas were published in *90 Tracts for the Times* (1833–41). A leading Tractarian was John Newman, vicar of St Mary's, who ultimately converted to Catholicism and became a cardinal. Oxford remains a major centre of High-Church Anglo-Catholicism to this day.

Leave the church and venture round onto the High Street to study the main entrance of St Mary's, the South Porch. Built in 1637, with its twisted columns, broken pediment and extravagant ornamentation, the porch bears all the hallmarks of the Italian Baroque, and was directly inspired by the canopy which had just been built by Bernini over the high altar of St Peter's in Rome.

Ⓔ Eating Out

Patisserie Valerie
90 High Street; tel: 01865 725 415; www.patisserie-valerie.co.uk; Mon–Sat 8am–7pm, Sun 9am–7pm. Smart café serving breakfast all day and salads and other lighter meals from lunchtime onwards. It is the cakes and pastries, however, that are this outfit's speciality. £–££

Quod Restaurant and Bar
92–4 High Street; tel: 01865 202 505; www.quod.co.uk; daily 7am–11pm. A stylish and bustling brasserie-style establishment, offering a varied menu with an Italian slant. It is particularly worth visiting during the week between the hours of noon and 7pm, when an excellent-value set-lunch menu (£) is available. Children are welcome here. ££–£££

Vaults and Garden Café
Vaults of the University Church, entrance from Radcliffe Square; tel: 01865 279 112; www.thevaults andgarden.com; daily 8.30am–6.30pm.
This informal café-restaurant serves soups, salads, sandwiches, cakes and other snacks daily. £

Above: the Quod Restaurant facade on the High Street.

Music and Theatre

With homespun performers from New College Choir to Radiohead and productions from Legally Blonde the Musical to Shakespeare, there is never a cultural drought in Oxford

MUSIC

The city is one of the finest in the country in terms of the quality and quantity of chamber and choral music it offers. The main concert venues for classical music are the Sheldonian Theatre (see p.16), the 250-seater Holywell Music Room (see p.32) and the Jacqueline du Pré Music Building. The city's churches and its college chapels provide further settings for concerts. The choirs of New College, Magdalen and Christ Church have strong reputations and can be heard for free at Choral Evensong, held most evenings in term time at about 6pm. Throughout the university year (Oct–June), the organisation Music at

Oxford puts on around 20 classical concerts at venues across the city, some with internationally renowned artists.

The city is no slouch in the rock stakes either, having spawned Radiohead and Supergrass. The main gig venue is the O2 Academy, while many pubs, like the Jericho Tavern, host live music. Freud bar (see p.95), in a grand neoclassical church, is great for jazz.

THEATRE

The main theatre, the Oxford Playhouse, has a programme of mostly modern theatre, music and dance; it also runs the intimate Burton Taylor Studio. Musical threatre, stand-up comedy and

Venues and Organisations

Sheldonian Theatre: tel: 01865 277 299; www.sheldon.ox.ac.uk

Holywell Music Room: tel: 01865 276 133; www.music.ox.ac.uk/facilities/Holywell-music-room.html. Coffee concerts held most Sundays at 11.15am (www.coffeeconcerts.com).

Jacqueline du Pré Music Building: tel: 01865 286 660; www.st-hildas. ox.ac.uk

Music at Oxford: tel: 01865 244 806; www.musicatoxford.com. Tickets also available from the Oxford Playhouse.

New College Choir: tel: 01865 279 519; www.newcollegechoir.com

Christ Church Cathedral and Choir: tel: 01865 276 150; www.chch. ox.ac.uk

Magdalen College Choir: tel: 01865 276 000; www.magd.ox.ac.uk/chapel-and-choir

O2 Academy: 190 Cowley Road; tel: 01865 813 500; www.o2academy oxford.co.uk

The Jericho Tavern: 56 Walton Street; tel: 01865 311 775

Freud: Walton Street; tel: 01865 311 171; www.freud.eu

Oxford Playhouse: Beaumont Street; tel: 01865 305 305; ww 01865 320 760 w.oxfordplayhouse.com

Burton Taylor Studio: Gloucester Street; tel: 01865 305 305; www. oxfordplayhouse.com

New Theatre: George Street; tel: 01865 320 760; www.newtheatre oxford.org.uk

The North Wall Arts Centre: South Parade; tel: 01865 319 450; www.thenorthwall.org

Old Fire Station: George Street; tel: 01865 263 980

Creation Theatre Co.: tel: 01865 766 266; www.creationtheatre.co.uk

gigs are staged at the New Theatre. For Shakespeare fans, a few colleges, notably Magdalen and Worcester, stage outdoor productions in summer. In addition, the Creation Theatre Company puts on a summer Shakespeare programme in settings such as the Oxford Castle courtyard, college gardens and the Saïd Business School amphitheatre. The Old Fire Station puts on art exhibits, theatre and music, as does the North Wall Arts Centre in Summertown.

Above: *The Taming of the Shrew* by the Creation Theatre Company. **Top Left**: the New Theatre Auditorium. **Bottom Left**: night performance at Oxford Castle.

Tour 2

Around New College

This half-day, 1-mile (1.6km) walk takes in the full span of Oxford's fascinating history, from a pagan Saxon well to the birthplace of Morris cars

Highlights

- Bridge of Sighs
- New College
- St Edmund Hall
- St Cross Church
- Holywell Music Room

Above: cycling under the Bridge of Sighs. **Below**: the Oxford coat of arms.

This route takes you on a loop around the northeastern part of the Old Town. Here, you can find arguably the oldest academic institution in Oxford (St Edmund's), as well as one of the newest (St Catherine's), and along the way take in some characterful old pubs and cafés for those all-important pitstops.

NEW COLLEGE LANE

The starting point of the walk is the **Bridge of Sighs ❶** – an anglicised version of the Venice original – which links the two parts of Hertford College. Pass under the bridge and into the dark and narrow New College Lane. This lane is a legacy of the replanning of the northeast quarter of the town in the late 14th-century, when many early-medieval dwellings were replaced by residential colleges. The original street pattern was obliterated, leaving New College Lane to wind its way between the high college walls.

Immediately on the left, almost beneath the Bridge of Sighs, you'll see a narrow opening – St Helen's Passage. This leads through to the **Turf Tavern** (see p.33). This cosy, low-beamed English pub is an Oxford legend. Its foundations date to the 13th century, though most of the present building is 16th-century. At the back is an attractive beer garden, and along the alleyway at the front is another terraced area, tucked up against the exterior wall of New College cloisters, with braziers for keeping warm in winter together with a hot rum punch.

HALLEY'S HOUSE

Back on New College Lane, a little further on and also on the left, you'll find a plaque on a house wall indicating that this was once the **home of astronomer Edmund Halley** (1656–1742). Halley calculated the orbit of the comet which now bears his name and his meteorological observations led to

Oxford's Ghosts

Walking down New College Lane at night, don't be surprised to hear the sound of horses' hooves ringing on the cobblestones and steel weapons clashing. In the Civil War, New College Lane was the assembly point for a Royalist force preparing to ride out from the city and confront Cromwell's Parliamentarians. Ghost experts maintain that their psychic energy lives on in those high walls. This and other spooky places feature on Bill Spectre's Ghost Trail (every Fri, Sat and Sun at 6.30pm, leaving from Oxford Castle Unlocked, and passing Oxford Tourist Information Centre on Broad Street at 7pm for a shorter tour; www.ghosttrail.org).

the publication in 1686 of the first map of the winds of the globe. He was appointed Astronomer Royal in 1720. A former pupil at Queen's College, Halley was appointed Savilan Professor of Geometry at Oxford in 1703. He built an observatory at his home here, which is still visible on the roof.

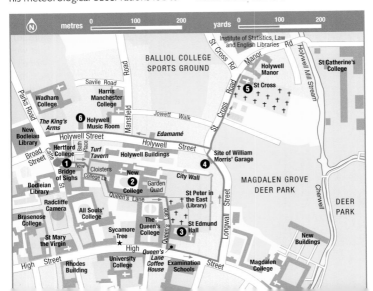

NEW COLLEGE

Soon, the lane turns sharp right, between the cloister walls of New College on the left and the barn that forms the lodgings of the college's warden (or head) on the right. Round another bend and straight ahead, you finally come to the gate-tower of **New College ❷** (tel: 01865 279 500; www.new. ox.ac.uk; March–mid-Oct daily 11am–5pm, charge; winter months: access only via gate on Holywell Street, *see p.32*, daily 2–4pm, free).

Established in 1379 by William of Wykeham, Bishop of Winchester, whose statue adorns the right-hand niche, New College was the very first college in Oxford to accept undergraduates. It was also purpose-built rather than built piecemeal like earlier colleges, and the design of the Front Quadrangle and surrounding buildings set a pattern that was followed by all subsequent college foundations.

Chapel and cloisters

The **chapel**, to the left of the gate-tower, is a fine example of the English Perpendicular style, though the roof and reredos are 19th-century restorations. In the ante-chapel, beneath

the great west window by Sir Joshua Reynolds, is the dramatic statue of *Lazarus* by Jacob Epstein (1951).

From the chapel, enter the **cloisters**, the last part of the original college buildings to be completed (in 1400). Dominated by an ancient ilex tree in one corner, the cloisters have a serene atmosphere, and are largely unchanged since the time they were built; the original wagon roof covers the passage.

In the northwest corner of the Front Quad, steps lead up into the

❶ Spoonerisms

The Reverend William Spooner (1844–1930) was elected warden of New College in 1903. His renown, however, rests on his habit of transposing the initial letters of words, which gave rise to 'Spoonerisms'. Examples of his gaffes include 'the Lord is our shoving leopard', and he once expelled an undergraduate with the words 'Sir, you have tasted two whole worms, you have hissed my mystery lectures and you were found fighting a liar in the quad: you will leave at once by the town drain.'

Above: Spooner lectured on ancient history, divinity and philosophy.

Above: the remains of the meticulously preserved medieval town wall in New College gardens.

Muniment Tower, providing access to the Hall, where portraits above the high table include that of William Spooner *(see box opposite)*.

Gardens
Outside again and through the archway you'll reach the **Garden Quad**, lined with 17th- and 18th-century college

Above: the fine wrought-iron screen marking the entrance to the gardens is a replica of the 1711 original.

buildings and enclosed at the western end by a fine wrought-iron screen giving access to the gardens themselves. As well as a decorative mound, the garden contains a substantial stretch of the **city's medieval wall**, which dates from 1226 when the original timber defensive walls of the town were rebuilt. When the founder secured the land on which to build the college, he also accepted responsibility for the upkeep of this part of the city wall, and even now, every three years the wall is inspected by the Lord Mayor to ensure that this obligation is being fulfilled. As a result, it is one of England's best-preserved examples of a town wall.

QUEEN'S LANE
Exit New College via the New College Lane gatehouse, and turn left under the archway and round another bend into Queen's Lane. On your left, the otherwise featureless wall of New College is embellished by a string course of delightful animal sculptures, created in the 1960s by Michael Groser. Beyond the sharp bend in the lane is the **Church of St Peter in the East**,

Above: the Front Quad of St Edmund Hall, the only surviving example in Oxford of the medieval halls that pre-dated the foundation of the colleges.

with its 11th-century tower – one of the oldest in Oxford. Originally dating from Saxon times, the present church is now the library of neighbouring St Edmund Hall, but visitors can at least gain access to the cavernous medieval crypt, one of the finest in the city, by asking for the key at St Edmund's porter's lodge. A gravestone in the churchyard commemorates James Sadler, described as the 'first English aeronaut', whose pioneering balloon flight took off from Christ Church Meadow on 4 October 1784.

ST EDMUND HALL

Continuing down Queen's Lane towards the High Street is the entrance to **St Edmund Hall** ❸ (tel: 01865 279 000; www.seh.ox.ac.uk; daily 10am–4pm, college functions permitting; free). Though it only achieved independent status as late as 1957, this tiny college is considered Oxford's oldest surviving educational establishment. Tradition has it that St Edmund of Abingdon founded it as an academic hall back in the 1190s, long before the first colleges were established in the city.

Set around small, flower-filled quads, everything about St Edmund Hall is on a diminutive scale, including the chapel, on the east side of the Front Quad, where fans of Pre-Raphaelite artists William Morris and Edward Burne-Jones can see some of their stained-glass work, together with original cartoon drawings (check at the lodge for permission to enter).

Above: do as the locals and cycle.

Above: the Church of St Cross' 13th-century tower and sundial clock.

Turn left here and continue as far as the traffic lights, beyond which lies Magdalen College, with its famous tower *(see p.61)*. Turn left again into Longwall Street. On your left at No. 48 is the building that housed **William Morris' Garage ❹**, where he built the prototype of the 'bullnose' Morris Oxford in 1912, a project that was to launch Morris on the road to fame and fortune, and launch Oxford into the industrial era. It was only a year later that Morris built his car plant out at Cowley, to the southeast of the city. Though the garage was converted into residential accommodation in 1981, there is a display window with further details on the career of Morris, who later became Lord Nuffield *(see also p.77)*.

THE LONGWALL GARAGE

The tranquillity of Queen's Lane comes to an abrupt end as you emerge on to the High Street. Immediately on the right stands The Queen's College *(see p.59)*, while on the corner on the left you'll find the Queen's Lane Coffee House *(see Eating Out, p.33)*, a venerable institution established back in 1654, where students still linger for hours over hearty breakfasts and mugs of coffee.

CHURCH OF ST CROSS

Next on the left is Holywell Street, but before walking up it, continue just a little further north along Longwall Street, which presently becomes St Cross Road, in order to see the **Church of St Cross ❺** on the right. The present church was founded in the 11th century on the site of an ancient chapel of St Peter in the East *(see p.29)*, which was established beside a pagan Saxon holy well (hence

⑤ The Wind in the Willows

The churchyard of St Cross contains some interesting graves, including those of Kenneth Grahame, author of *The Wind in the Willows*, and the Oxford shopkeeper Theophilus Carter, reputedly the model for Lewis Carroll's Mad Hatter in *Alice in Wonderland*. Carter made his living selling furniture, though he was more renowned for his eccentric inventions, including the 'Alarm Clock Bed' which at waking-time tipped its occupant out into a tub of cold water.

Above: Ratty and Mole of *The Wind in the Willows* fame.

Above: the King's Arms on Holywell Street is so often spilling out with students that it is practically part of the university.

'Holywell'), and became an important place of pilgrimage. The only surviving Norman part of the church is the chancel, but the 13th-century tower has a fascinating sundial clock. The key to the church is available from the porter of the neighbouring Holywell Manor; sadly, the ancient holy well is no longer there.

Opposite Holywell Manor are the huge brick cubes of the Law Library (1964), and if you continue along Manor Road, you will arrive at **St Catherine's College**, which was designed by Danish architect Arne Jacobsen and completed in 1964. While modern architects rave over its pioneering 'functional' style, most find the plain yellow-brick buildings dull. However, the landscaping, also planned by Jacobsen, is now mature and does much to compensate – especially the long vista between the Cherwell and the water gardens, backed by the splendid trees of Magdalen College meadows.

HOLYWELL STREET

Now retrace your steps to Holywell Street. This cobbled road marks a clear boundary between cluttered Old Oxford and much later developments to the north. One of the most delightful streets in the city, it is lined by pastel-coloured 17th- and 18th-century houses, as well as New College's imposing Holywell Buildings on the left-hand side.

Towards the end of the street, on the right, standing back from the road, is the **Holywell Music Room** ❻,

Above: The Holywell Music Room has acoustics that do particular justice to solo recitals and chamber concerts.

which was opened in 1748 and is said to be the world's oldest surviving concert hall. Regular recitals and chamber concerts are held here in an auditorium that once saw Haydn perform.

BATH PLACE

Opposite the Music Room is **Bath Place**, a narrow, cobbled alley providing access to a ramshackle collection of old buildings, including the Bath Place Hotel *(see p.125)*, and, after a sharp turn, the Turf Tavern, a splendid low-beamed English tavern *(see below)*. Holywell Street ends back in Broad Street opposite the massive 1930s-style New Bodleian Library; on the corner of Holywell Street and Parks Road is **The King's Arms**, a pub much frequented by students, particularly in June when they gather here to celebrate the end of their exams *(see below)*.

Above: St Edmund Hall.

Holywell Street

E Eating Out

Edamamé
15 Holywell Street; tel: 01865 246 916; www.edamame.co.uk; lunch Wed–Sun, dinner Fri–Sat 5–8.30pm (last orders), usually closed during Sept.
This Japanese restaurant is a little gem. If you can work around the eccentric opening times, you will not be disappointed with the quality of the food, and the prices are remarkably low. On Thursday evenings, the menu consists entirely of sushi. Caters for meat-eaters, pescatorians and vegetarians. £

The King's Arms
40 Holywell Street; tel: 01865 242 369; www.youngs.co.uk; daily 10.30am–midnight, food served 11.30am–9.30pm.
This pub has been in operation since 1607, and the King's Arms in question are those of James I. Nowadays it is owned by Young's Brewery, and though this is not the subtlest of

venues – the food and beer are very much standard pub fare – the atmosphere is always convivial, particularly in the snug back rooms. £

The Queen's Lane Coffee House
40 High Street; tel: 01865 240 082; Mon–Sat 7.30am–8pm, Sun 9am–8pm.
A perennial student favourite, this convenient café has just been refurbished. It does, however, still serve good snacks, light lunches and cream teas, just as it always has. £

The Turf Tavern
Tel: 01865 243 235; www.theturftavern. co.uk; Mon–Sat 11am–11pm, Sun noon–10.30pm, food served daily 11am–9pm.
This ancient pub serves some of the best beer in Oxford. The food is traditional and hearty, though a definite cut above the average pub standard. The wonderful interior is intimate, but there is also plenty of outside seating, with braziers lit in the winter. £

Tour 3

Where Town Meets Gown

This half-day's walk of less than a mile around the old commercial district of central Oxford offers plenty to interest sightseers, shoppers and gourmets alike

This route straddles the boundaries between town and gown, highlighting the abiding contrast between the cloistral hush of the college quadrangles and the commercial bustle of the city streets.

MARTYRS' MEMORIAL

The walk begins at the southern end of St Giles', where the **Martyrs' Memorial** ❶ was erected by public subscription in 1841–3, according to designs by Sir George Gilbert Scott. The martyrs in question were Bishops Latimer, Ridley and Cranmer, now collectively known as the Oxford Martyrs. They were the most high-profile victims of the Catholic Queen Mary's purge of Protestants, and were burned at the stake in the town's

> ### Highlights
> - Martyrs' Memorial
> - Trinity College
> - Blackwell's Bookshop
> - Exeter College Chapel
> - Covered Market
> - Carfax

north ditch, now Broad Street, just around the corner (a cross marked in the road surface opposite Balliol College shows the exact site). Latimer and Ridley went to the stake first, in 1555, followed by Cranmer in 1556. An inscription on the monument states that they died for maintaining sacred truths 'against the errors of the Church of Rome'.

Left: Trinity College and its inviting, open lawn. **Above**: neo-Gothic Martyrs' Memorial.

Above: Bishop Latimer.

Immediately to the south of the Martyrs' Memorial is the **Church of St Mary Magdalen**, a centre of Anglo-Catholicism whose congregation remains loyal to the memory of Charles I, celebrating the Feast of King Charles the Martyr on 30 January.

BROAD STREET

Broad Street is aptly named, though it was originally known as Horsemongers Street after a horse fair held here just outside the city walls from 1235. Narrow at each end and wide in the middle, it has a feeling of spaciousness, enhanced by view on to the lawns of Trinity College on the north side, which are separated from the street only by a wrought-iron gate. The far end is dominated by the Sheldonian Theatre and Clarendon Building (see p.15), and much of the south side is distinguished by its colourful façades above some interesting shops, including Oxfam (Oxford Committee for Famine Relief), the first shop to be opened by the charity in 1948.

The **Oxford Information Centre** (tel: 01865 252 200; Mon–Sat 9.30am–5pm, Sun 10am–4pm) is situated at 15–16 Broad Street, adjacent to Oxfam. Advice and leaflets can be obtained here, as well as bookings made

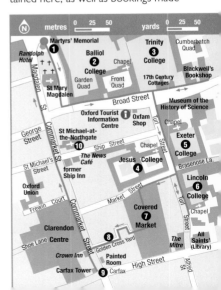

for guided walking tours. You can also hop aboard a sightseeing bus just opposite *(see p.124)*.

BALLIOL COLLEGE

On the other side of the street stands **Balliol College** ❷ (tel: 01865 277 777; www.balliol.ox.ac.uk; daily 10am–5pm; charge) renowned for having produced a greater number of politicians and statesmen than any other college in Oxford. They include Chris Patten (present Chancellor of the University) as well as former prime ministers Harold Macmillan and Edward Heath. Together with University College and Merton, Balliol claims to be the oldest college in Oxford, said to have been founded in 1263 by John Balliol, as penance for insulting the Bishop of Durham. Little of the present college dates from this time, however; Balliol was rebuilt in Victorian times with wealth generated by its coal-rich estates in Northumbria.

Above: Balliol College facade.

TRINITY COLLEGE

Adjacent to Balliol, **Trinity College** ❸ (tel: 01865 279 900; www.trinity.ox.ac.uk; Mon–Fri & Sat–Sun during vacations 10.30am–noon, 2–4pm, Sat–Sun term time 2–4pm; charge) dates back to 1286, when monks from Durham Abbey founded a college on the site of the present-day Durham Quad. After the Dissolution, Sir Thomas Pope rescued the property and refounded the college in 1555.

Unlike most other Oxford colleges, the front quad is not closed off from the street, and its lawn almost invites visitors to enter, which they do through a small entrance between the wrought-iron gate and a row of humble 17th-century cottages (rebuilt in 1969). Apart from the baroque chapel, with its splendidly carved wooden panelling, stalls, screen, and reredos, the principal attraction of Trinity is its fine gardens, entered through a wrought-iron screen from the Garden Quad. Extending to Parks Road, they provide a wonderful feeling of spaciousness.

BLACKWELL'S

Back on Broad Street, next door to Trinity and diagonally opposite the Sheldonian is **Blackwell's**, one of the world's most famous bookshops. Opened in 1879 by Benjamin Henry Blackwell, the original shop was tiny, just 12ft (3.6m) square, and was criticised by many for its situation.

Blackwell's gradually expanded, however, in order to meet the steadily increasing volume of business and took over more space behind the shop. Today the initial impression is of a large provincial bookshop. In the basement, however, is the cavernous Norrington Room, a huge space that extends under Trinity College and is packed from floor to ceiling with around 160,000 volumes on over three miles of shelving. When the room was opened in

Above: Blackwell's on Broad Sreet is an Oxford icon and one of the most famous bookshops in the world.

1966, it gained a place in the Guinness Book of Records for having the largest display of books for sale in one room anywhere in the world.

The pre-eminence of Blackwell's in Oxford is reflected not only here, but in its other premises in the city, including the Art and Poster Shop on the other side of Broad Street (corner of Turl Street), and the Music Shop (on the opposite corner).

TURL STREET

Now continue the walk by turning off Broad Street on to shady Turl Street, which cuts through towards the High Street. 'The Turl' is thought to derive its name from a pedestrian turnstile or twirling gate set into the medieval wall that once ran along the southern side of Broad Street. Today it forms a distinct boundary between town and gown, with most of the central colleges and the heart of the university lying to the east, and the city's shops and markets to the west.

The exception that proves the rule is **Jesus College ❹** (tel: 01865 279 700; www.jesus.ox.ac.uk; daily 2–4.30pm; free), a short way down on the right (west). Jesus is also known as the Welsh college, because the money for its foundation in 1571 was provided

Ⓢ Retail Therapy

There are many opportunities for shopping along this route. Apart from the food shops in the Covered Market, emporia to look out for include Ducker & Son at No. 6 Turl Street, which have been selling hand-made shoes of the highest quality for generations; the Whisky Shop, just next door at No. 7; Scriptum also on Turl Street, at No. 3, an old-fashioned shop crammed with pens, quills and leather-bound notebooks; an excellent artists' materials shops called Broad Canvas at No. 20 Broad Street; and Collector's Corner, selling toy cars from a shop just inside the entrance of the Market Street entrance of the Covered Market (unit 130).

Above: Oxford offers an intriguing mixture of traditional and modern shops catering for every taste.

Above: Exeter College and its impressive chapel, viewed from the top of the Church of St Mary the Virgin.

by a Welshman called Hugh Price, and much of its intake was from the grammar schools of Wales. The college retains its strong Welsh links, though two of its most famous alumni, Harold Wilson and T.E. Lawrence were non-Welsh. Commemorated by a bust in the chapel, the latter spent little time in the college, preferring to study medieval military architecture in a shed in the garden of his parents' house at No. 2 Polstead Road in North Oxford.

EXETER COLLEGE

Opposite Jesus College is **Exeter College** ❺ (tel: 01865 279 600; www.exeter.ox.ac.uk; daily 2–5pm; free), founded in 1314, which is particularly well worth visiting for the magnificent chapel that dominates the first quadrangle. This was built in 1854–60 to the design of Sir George Gilbert Scott, and is an almost direct copy of the French High Gothic style as seen in the Sainte Chapelle in Paris. The stained glass is magnificent, as is the mosaic work of the apse. To the right of the altar, visitors will also see the large tapestry of the *Adoration of*

the Magi, made in 1890 to a design by the Pre-Raphaelite artist Edward Burne-Jones, who had studied at Exeter together with William Morris.

Another highlight of Exeter is the Fellows Garden, accessed through a doorway to the rear of the front quad.

Above: magnificent carved wooden door leading into Exeter College.

The fine chestnut trees here were much enjoyed by J.R.R. Tolkien (1892–1973), author of *The Lord of the Rings*, who was a student at Exeter and now lies buried in Wolvercote Cemetery, North Oxford. He no doubt also enjoyed the magnificent view from the top of the garden wall, which provides a fresh perspective of Radcliffe Square (see p.19); you feel you can almost reach out and touch the Radcliffe Camera, with the towers of All Souls and St Mary the Virgin looming behind.

LINCOLN COLLEGE

Further down Turl Street on the left is **Lincoln College** ❻ (tel: 01865 279 800; www.lincoln.ox.ac.uk; Mon–Fri 2–5pm, Sat–Sun 11am–5pm; free). It was founded in 1427 by the Bishop of Lincoln, Richard Fleming, but he died four years later, leaving the college with little income and few endowments. As a result, the college retains much of its original fabric – notably the front quad – since it has never experienced the kind of alterations and 'improvements' undertaken by

Above: quiet study time in Lincoln's high-ceilinged library.

wealthier colleges. The Chapel Quad to the south was added in the early 17th century, and the chapel itself contains fine carved woodwork as well as exquisite stained glass by the prolific German artist Abraham von Linge, who arrived in Oxford in 1629 and proceeded to leave his mark on

Ⓚ Father of Fantasy

J.R.R. Tolkien's long association with Oxford began as a student in 1911 and went on to include a spell working at the Oxford English Dictionary (fifty years later an entry for 'hobbit' was added) and a teaching career lasting from 1925 to 1959. Though he had long been inventing languages and writing on the history and myth of Middle Earth, it was not until 1937 that *The Hobbit* was published. *The Lord of the Rings* followed in 1954 and by the mid-1960s had achieved cult status. The Oxford Information Centre at 15–16 Broad Street (tel: 01865 252 200) organises walking tours dedicated to sites of interest to Tolkien fans.

Above: Tolkien specialised in Old English at Exeter College.

Above: taking in the sights from the top of Carfax Tower.

other college chapels as well, in particular, University and Queen's (see p.58). During the 18th century, Lincoln College became a meeting place for the so-called Holy Club, which, under the leadership of John Wesley, grew into the great evangelical movement known as Methodism.

COVERED MARKET

Returning back up Turl Street, now turn left (west) on to Market Street, which takes you to the north entrance of the **Covered Market** ❼ (Mon–Sat 9am–5.30pm, Sun 10am–4pm). Established by the Paving Commission in 1774 as a permanent home for the many stall-holders cluttering the city streets, this is an Oxford institution that should not be missed, especially if you're visiting around Christmas, when the market becomes a spectacular tribute to gastronomic excess.

The central range is dominated by the butchers, whose fronts – particularly during the festive season – are hung with an astonishing variety of carcasses, from rabbits and hares to wild boar and even deer. There are also greengrocers, a cheesemonger and a cake shop, shops selling sausages, pasties, meat pies and sandwiches, as well as tea shops, all vying for custom alongside smart boutiques, gift shops and florists. It is also the home of the original Ben's Cookies shop, where American-style cookies are baked on the premises, and there are several places selling snacks and lunches (see Eating Out, p.43), all providing welcome escape from the bustle outside.

Above: the Covered Market retains its turn-of-the-century atmosphere.

GOLDEN CROSS YARD

You can exit the Covered Market either on to the High Street, or else via an arcade on the west side and into the beautifully restored **Golden Cross Yard** ❸. Now occupied by a café, pizza restaurant, jewellery and clothes boutiques and a health food store, the courtyard was originally created in the Middle Ages for the Cross Inn; indeed, an inn may have existed on this site as early as 1193. In the 16th century it was used by travelling companies of players. The first floor of the Pizza Express restaurant occupies the former bedroom accommodation of the inn and contains the fragments of two painted rooms, the Crown Chamber and the Prince's Chamber. The bishops Latimer and Ridley were cross-examined here in 1555 while imprisoned at the nearby Bocardo *(see p.43)*.

CARFAX

Continuing through an archway, you now emerge into the rather less intimate atmosphere of central Oxford. Severely blemished by the wholesale destruction of many of its fine buildings, commercial Cornmarket Street, which was pedestrianised in 1999 and repaved at huge expense in 2002–4, is the city's main shopping thoroughfare. Yet the street does retain some historic attractions.

The busy crossroads at the southern end is known as **Carfax** ❾, after the Norman 'Quatre Voies' (four ways). This is the ancient heart of Saxon Oxford, where the four roads from north, south, east and west met. Carfax still remains the focal point of the town. Its prime attraction is the Carfax Tower *(see box right)* – all that remains of the 13th-century St Martin's Church, which was pulled down as part of a road-widening scheme in 1896, and was itself built on the site of an earlier, late-Saxon church. The

legend of St Martin giving his cloak to a beggar is portrayed in a sculpture occupying a niche in the archway adjacent to the tower; today, the archway has the more profane function of providing access to a sandwich bar.

Also on Carfax stood the Swindlestock Tavern, where, on St Scholastica's Day (10 February) 1355, an argument between scholars and the landlord developed into a full-blown riot resulting in the deaths of many scholars. The site of the tavern is indicated by a plaque on the wall of the Abbey Bank.

Ⓥ Carfax Tower

Carfax Tower can be climbed for fine views of the city (daily, Apr–Sept 10am–5.30pm, Nov–Feb 10am–3pm, Oct 10am–4.30pm, March 10am–4pm; charge). The east side of the tower is embellished with quarterboys which strike the bell every 15 minutes (they are replicas of those taken from the original church) as well as the original church clock.

Above: the clock and quarterboys on Carfax Tower.

Above: the now pedestrianised Cornmarket Street is Oxford's main shopping throughfare, featuring the usual high-street names.

PAINTED ROOM

Proceeding up Cornmarket from Carfax, No. 3 is the site of the Crown Tavern, in which William Shakespeare reputedly stayed on his journeys between London and Stratford. Although changed almost beyond recognition in the 1920s, the **Painted Room** on the second floor has well-preserved Elizabethan wall paintings of fruits and flowers. The room is now a private office, but the design can be viewed by appointment through the Oxford Preservation Trust (tel: 01865 242 918).

ST MICHAEL-AT-THE-NORTHGATE

Continue along Cornmarket until you get to the corner of Ship Street. Here, the former Ship Inn, a fine medieval building, was restored by Jesus College before being taken over by retailers. Just opposite stands the oldest surviving stone structure in Oxford, the late-Saxon tower of the church of **St Michael-at-the-Northgate** ❿, which was built in around 1040 as a look-out against the Danes (daily 10.30am–5pm; charge).

In the late 18th century, the old North Gate itself, part of the fortifications of Edward the Elder's original Saxon town, was dismantled by the Paving Commission. Prior to that, in 1293, the tower had been connected

Above: the Saxon tower of St Michael-at-the-Northgate is Oxford's oldest surviving building.

on its west side to the Bocardo prison above the North Gate; it was here that in 1555 the Oxford Martyrs, Cranmer, Ridley and Latimer (see p.22) were imprisoned before being taken to be burned at the stake in Broad Street; the opening for the cell door can still be seen in the side of the tower.

St Michael's itself is mentioned in the Domesday Book, but the oldest part of the present church dates from the 13th century; above the altar, the medallions in the windows are the oldest examples of stained glass in Oxford, dating from 1290. The font is from the 14th century, and Shakespeare is known to have stood by it as a godparent to the child of a Cornmarket innkeeper. Charles I attended services here during the Civil War.

BACK TO THE START

Continuing north past the Waterstones bookshop, Cornmarket ends and Magdalen Street begins. The church of St Mary Magdalen is on your right and the Randolph Hotel on your left as before long you arrive back at the Martyrs' Memorial.

E Eating Out

Brown's Café
Avenue 4, Covered Market; tel: 01865 233 436; Mon–Sat 8.30am–5.30pm.
This cheap and cheerful greasy spoon – which does not appear to have changed much since the 1950s (and in that retro way, is now quite stylish) – serves all-day breakfasts, sandwiches, and incongruously, a number of Portuguese dishes. £

The Crown Inn
59a Cornmarket; tel: 01865 813 961; daily 11am–11pm.
This is a rare reminder of what the historic Cornmarket Street once looked like. Tucked away behind modern buildings, the Elizabethan-era pub, with a good-value menu, is a civilised place for lunch or an early evening drink. £

Georgina's
Avenue 3, Covered Market; tel: 01865 249 527; daily 8.30am–5pm.
Situated in the Covered Market, Georgina's caters to a youthful health-conscious crowd, serving organic and mostly vegetarian food as well as delicious cakes in a cosy upstairs retreat that tends to fill up quickly at lunchtimes. £

The News Café
1 Ship Street; tel: 01865 242 317; daily 9am–9pm.

As its name implies, this café aims to keep its visitors up to date with the news as well as refreshed. Newspapers and TV screens galore should satisfy the most avid news junkie, while the menu, ranging from big breakfasts to pasta and salads, is just the business. £–££

Pieminister
Avenue 2, Covered Market; tel: 01865 241 613; www.pieminister. co.uk; Mon–Sat 9.30am–5pm.
This smart little outfit concentrates on the pie, in all its forms. Pies come with a wide variety of fillings (including vegetarian ones), and there are mash, peas and gravy to keep them company. £

Above: save space for dessert.

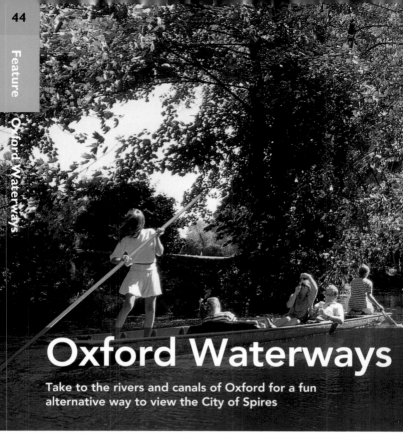

Oxford Waterways

Take to the rivers and canals of Oxford for a fun alternative way to view the City of Spires

Oxford's three waterways, the Thames (known here as the Isis), its major tributary the Cherwell (pronounced 'Charwell') and the canal provide not only a different perspective on the city but also an escape into rural surroundings right on its doorstep.

THE CHERWELL

Noted for its absence of rowing crews and power boats, the Cherwell is much more tranquil than the Thames and is hence the preferred river for punting or rowing skiffs. Its peaceful narrow backwaters can be followed all the way up to the village of Islip to the north, but the Victoria Arms on the way (at Old Marston) is a well-known landing stage. Traditional Thames river craft, punts were originally used by the watermen for fishing and ferrying. Novices may have initial difficulties using the pole to steer and propel the punt, but a paddle is supplied in case the pole gets stuck in the mud or you veer towards the riverbank. Punts (chauffeured or not) and rowing boats can be hired from the Cherwell Boathouse, Bardwell Road (tel: 01865 515 978; www.cherwellboathouse.co.uk), from Magdalen

THE THAMES (ISIS)

Visitors can enjoy the Thames at Christ Church Meadow, through which a wide, tree-lined, well maintained track leads down to the waterfront and, to the east, to a long chain of college boathouses. This stretch comes alive during 'Eights Week', held from the Wednesday to the Saturday of the fifth week of Trinity (summer) term. Eight-oared crews from all colleges compete for the distinction of being 'head' of the river. The boat that crosses the finishing line without being 'bumped' (overtaken) is the winner, but any crew that successfully bumps five or more other boats throughout the week is awarded 'blades', meaning that each crew member can buy their own commemorative oar. Pimm's and barbecued food are sold down by the boathouses, making Eights Week a sociable affair.

Near Christ Church Meadow is Folly Bridge (the Head of the River pub – *see p.75* – is a popular drinking hole here), where Salter's Steamers Ltd *(see above)* offers cruises along the river to the village of Iffley and to Abingdon. Iffley can also be reached by following the towpath; it is worth visiting for the historic church of St Mary the Virgin. The interior of the Isis Tavern on the opposite bank brims with university boating regalia.

Another good place to enjoy the Thames is at Port Meadow *(see p.104)*, north of Oxford via Walton Street and the district of Jericho. The walk along the riverbank leads to the village of Binsey, with its pub, the Perch, and continues all the way to another historic inn, the Trout *(see p.107)* at Godstow.

THE CANAL

Last but not least is the canal, a busy industrial waterway after its completion in 1790, but now a ribbon of tranquillity on the edge of the city, and home to many house boats. To explore it, take the towpath walk from Hythe Bridge Street to the north *(see p.80)*.

Bridge Boathouse (tel: 01865 202 643; www.oxfordpunting.co.uk), and from Salter's Steamers (tel: 01865 243 421; www.salterssteamers.co.uk) at Folly Bridge. The Cherwell can also be explored from dry land, in particular from the University Parks (accessible from Parks Road) and from Addison's Walk in the grounds of Magdalen College *(see p.61)*.

Above: punting on the tranquil waters of the Cherwell. **Top Right**: the Head of the River pub at Folly Bridge draws big crowds in the summer on account of its attractive terrace. **Bottom Right**: colourful canal boat. **Left**: rowing practice on the Isis.

Tour 4

Quads, Meadows and Gardens

This half-day, mile-long ramble around the colleges, meadows and gardens to the south of the High Street evokes a world of genteel rusticity

This tour begins at Carfax and heads east, but soon forsakes the High Street to discover an old tavern and some of the more venerable colleges before finishing at the lovely Botanic Garden. Merton College is especially important, as many of its features provided the model for later college foundations.

Highlights

- The Bear Pub
- Corpus Christi College Gardens
- Merton College Library and Chapel
- Christ Church Meadow
- Botanic Garden

ORIEL SQUARE

From Carfax *(see p.41)*, cross over to the south side of the High Street and proceed eastwards until you find the turning for Alfred Street on the right. At the bottom of this narrow lane is one of Oxford's oldest (and smallest) pubs, **The Bear ❶** *(see p.53)*, which dates from 1242. Its walls and ceiling are lined with cabinets containing over 7,000 ties from a huge range of organisations – mostly clubs and regiments.

After some refreshment, continue due east along Bear Lane to arrive in peaceful Oriel Square. Notice on the north side and in neighbouring Oriel Street the facades of the houses painted in bright Regency colours. Ranged along the east side

Left: the immaculate lawns of Magdalen College.

of the Square is **Oriel College** ❷ (tel: 01865 276 555; www.oriel.ox.ac.uk; daily 2–5pm), which was founded in 1324. Though it is not open in the summer term, visitors may be able to peek into the lavish, Jacobean-Gothic style front quad. Dominating the quad is the staircase entrance to the Hall, with its open strapwork cresting, and its inscription *Regnante Carolo* making a bold statement of Royalist support for Charles I. In the niches above are statues of Charles I and Edward II (during whose reign Oriel was founded), as well as a matronly Virgin and Child.

CORPUS CHRISTI COLLEGE

Leaving Oriel Square on the south side, proceed on to cobbled Merton Street. Just a short way along on the right is the entrance to **Corpus Christi College** ❸ (tel: 01865 276 700; www.ccc.ox.ac.uk; daily 1.30–4.30pm; free), founded by Richard Foxe, Bishop of Winchester, in 1517. Bishop Foxe intended the college to be a place of liberal education (hitherto unknown in Oxford), and he won praise from his humanist friend

ⓕ Bastion of Tradition

While Oxford colleges are often criticised for being stuck in the past, in fact, many are now fairly progressive institutions. Oriel College, however, would probably not be considered among the latter. It was the last college to admit female students, holding out until 1985. It is also known for the right-wing leanings of its undergraduates, having the only Junior Common Room in Oxford that refuses to subscribe to the university's student union. Another of its traditions is rowing: the college has dominated inter-college competitions on the river over the past few decades.

Above: the Jacobean-Gothic style front quad, Oriel College.

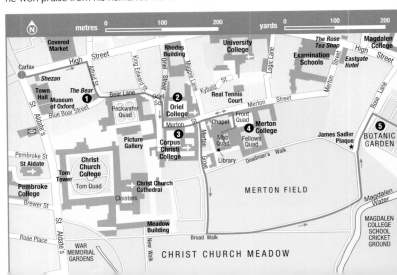

Above: Merton College Library is regarded as the finest example of a medieval library in the whole of England.

Erasmus for providing tuition in Greek as well as Latin.

The college's most famous landmark is the sundial in the front quad, which is inscribed on a tall column topped by the college's emblem. But visitors should not leave without also seeing the small college garden behind the Fellows' Building. Domi-

Above: The Bear is one of Oxford's oldest and smallest pubs.

nated by a magnificent copper beech, the garden provides a fine view of Christ Church Meadow, with the Fellows' Garden of Christ Church in the foreground. The view from the raised platform at the back is even better, and you can see down into the secretive Deanery Garden of Christ Church, where Charles Dodgson, alias Lewis Carroll, first got to know young Alice (see p.73).

MERTON COLLEGE

Beyond Corpus Christi, the street is dominated by the tower of the chapel of **Merton College** ❹ (tel: 01865 276310; www.merton.ox.ac.uk; Mon–Fri 2–5pm, Sat–Sun 10am–5pm; free). The gate-tower of Merton College itself is a little further along. Founded in 1264 by Walter de Merton, Lord Chancellor of England, the college is one of the oldest in Oxford. Like other early colleges, it was designed to be a highly exclusive institution, housing a small, privileged minority of mostly graduate fellows. The gate-tower has two niches, which contain the statues of the founder and King Henry III, who

Above: enjoying a game of cricket by Merton College.

was on the throne at the time; between them is an intricate relief portraying the *History of John the Baptist*.

Mob Quad and the Old Library

The front quad lacks the calm regularity of some other quads in the city. With buildings dating from the 13th to 19th centuries, it is typical of the piecemeal development of the early colleges. Nevertheless, Merton has some very special features that provided models for later foundations. Principal among these is **Mob Quad**, accessed by going through the arch to the right of the Hall and turning right. The oldest college quad in Oxford, its form is probably based on that of a medieval inn. The north and east ranges (for accommodation) were completed first, in 1311, followed by the south and west ranges, built to house the **Library**, regarded as the finest example of a medieval library in England (guided tours with the verger for a maximum of eight people July–Sept 2, 3 and 4pm, telephone ahead to check; charge).

You'll find the library entrance in the southwest corner of Mob Quad. The ancient oak door is believed to have been taken from Beaumont Palace, the royal palace of Henry I that once stood on Beaumont Street *(see p.89)*. The library itself is up a flight of stone steps. Though its medieval structure remains intact, substantial alterations were carried out subsequent to its completion in 1379. The

(see p.89)

F Real Tennis

Opposite the main gate of Merton College stands one of England's 25 Real Tennis courts. A court has existed on this site since the late 16th century, and the present court (which looks like a large barn from the outside) dates from the late 18th century. Real (probably derived from 'royal') Tennis differs from lawn tennis mainly in that it is played inside, with participants hitting the ball against the walls as well as over a net. The games roots go back to medieval monastery life. Visitors can go along and have a look between 9am and 6pm on weekdays (tel: 01865 244 212; charge).

Above: the tranquil Mob Quad of Merton College is the oldest college quad in Oxford.

Above: the enormous neo-Gothic Meadow Building of Christ Church marks the start of the delightful tree-lined New Walk.

wooden ceiling, for example, is Tudor, while the panelling and plasterwork date from the late 16th and early 17th centuries. Among the many exhibits is one of the locked chests in which the manuscripts were originally stored. Books came later, as did the bookshelves, a feature introduced from Italy and Germany.

The west wing is adjoined by the **Max Beerbohm Room**, full of drawings by the famous caricaturist (1872–1956), who studied at Merton

Above: Merton Street facades.

and wrote *Zuleika Dobson* (1911), a satire on Oxford undergraduate life.

The chapel

The chapel is definitely worth a visit. The choir (late 13th century) and transepts (14th–15th century) are, respectively, good examples of the English Decorated and Perpendicular architectural styles. The magnificent east window, with its fine tracery and original glass, is easily the most beautiful in Oxford. The original intention was to complete the building with a cathedral-scale nave, but this never came about, probably because of lack of funds and space. As a result the transept became the ante-chapel and the choir the chapel – another pattern that was to be repeated by later colleges.

The massive gargoyles that leer from the battlements are another example of brilliant modern masonry – put up in the 1960s to replace the eroded stumps of the originals. Further highlights of the chapel include a memorial, on the west wall, to Sir Thomas Bodley, founder of the great library that bears his name (see p.16).

Above: ceremony outside Merton College Chapel.

DEADMAN'S WALK

Leaving Merton College, retrace your steps back up Merton Street (westwards) as far as the wrought-iron gateway (daily until 7pm) on the left, between Merton College Chapel and Corpus Christi. Take the footpath – known as Merton Grove – and at the turnstile gateway at the end you emerge on to the broad expanse of Christ Church Meadow.

Immediately on the left is **Deadman's Walk**, which follows the old city wall to the east, round the back of Merton College. It was along this path that funerals once processed to the old Jewish cemetery, now the Botanic Garden (see p.52). If you follow this route, just before the path ends at Rose Lane you will see a plaque on the wall dedicated to the balloonist James Sadler, the 'first English aeronaut who in a fire balloon made a successful ascent from near this place on 4 October 1784 to land near Woodeaton'. The views experienced by Sadler as he rose above the meadow and the spires of Oxford must have been stunning.

CHRIST CHURCH MEADOW

For better views from ground level, instead of taking Deadman's Walk continue south from Merton Grove, past Christ Church Fellows' Garden, to the **Broad Walk**. To the right is the enormous neo-Gothic Meadow Building of Christ Church (see p.69), from where the delightful tree-lined New Walk provides a pleasant detour down past Christ Church Meadow to the River Thames and the Col-

G Protected Meadow

It is not actually possible to walk on Christ Church Meadow itself because it is fenced off to contain its herd of fine Long Horn cattle (you will probably see some of these beasts at close quarters as you walk down New Walk). But a stroll around it is well worthwhile, not only for giving a feeling of countryside so close to the city, but also for allowing the chance to see college boat crews sculling up and down the river, practising for 'Eights Week' and 'Torpids', the university's two main rowing competitions.

Above: taking it easy on Christ Church Meadow.

Above: the Broad Walk, in front of Christ Church.

lege Boathouses *(see p.75)*. The main route, however, turns left along Broad Walk, taking in fine views of the college skyline to the north before arriving at Magdalen Water, an arm of the tranquil River Cherwell.

BOTANIC GARDEN

Leaving Christ Church Meadow, continue on to Rose Lane at the eastern boundary of Merton College, and on the right is the side entrance to the **University Botanic Garden** ❺ (tel: 01865 286 690; www.botanic-garden.ox.ac.uk; daily May–Aug 9am–6pm, Mar–Apr, Sept–Oct 9am–5pm, Nov–Feb 9am–4pm; charge except on weekdays Nov–Feb). Founded in 1621 by Henry Danvers, Earl of Danby, as a physic garden for the growing of herbs and plants for use in medicine and science, this is the oldest botanic garden in Britain.

The garden layout

It was created on the site of the city's medieval Jewish cemetery, and much of the original layout, based on a series of rectangular beds, each devoted to one of the principal plant families, has survived. The garden, which covers an area of some 5 acres (2 hectares), is surrounded on three sides by a 14ft (4m) wall, built by the first keeper, a retired German soldier and publican named Jacob Bobart. The fourth side (aligned with the High Street) is enclosed by laboratory buildings and

Above: the Oxford Botanic Garden is the oldest in Britain.

the massive stone triumphal arch designed by Nicholas Stone as the main entrance in 1632 (the statues of Charles I, Charles II and the Earl of Danby were added later).

At the far end of the central path, on the right, is a huge yew tree, sole survivor of an avenue of yews planted in 1650 by Bobart, which in former times would have been clipped. Beyond, the triangular New Garden, enclosed in 1944, contains a lily pond, bog garden and two rockeries for lime-loving plants. Another part of the garden is planted with roses illustrating the development of hybrid varieties in the 19th and 20th centuries. From the central pond, the view through the arch to Magdalen tower on the other side is magnificent.

Visitors can also admire plants kept in the huge glasshouses built right next to the Cherwell. In winter, when the gardens can look a bit bleak, these glasshouses provide an instant change of climate as well as the sight of luxuri-

Above: the Garden also has some impressive glasshouses where tropical plants are grown.

ant palms and lotuses, ferns and alpines and a special collection of carnivorous plants. A stroll along the River Cherwell here is very pleasant and in summer it is crowded with punters.

E Eating Out

The Bear
6 Alfred Street; tel: 01865 728 164; daily 11am–11pm, food served noon–3pm and 6–9pm.
This wonderful pub is a haven for good beer and conversation. The historic interior is even more cramped than usual on Tuesday evenings, when quiz night is held. In the summer, however, seating is available outside too. £

Shezan
135 High Street; tel: 01865 251 600; www.shezanoxford.co.uk; daily noon–2.30pm (Fri–Sun till 3pm) and 5.30pm till late.
A cut above the usual Tandoori place, this centrally located and tastefully decorated place aims to recreate the spicy flavours of the Mughal dynasty. £–££

Eastgate Hotel
73 High Street; tel: 01865 248 695; www.thehightableoxford.co.uk; daily 7am–10pm. Located right at the east end of Merton Street, this hotel has a restaurant called the High Table Brasserie. Despite the pretensions of the name – college high tables (where Fellows dine) could not be less like brasseries – this is a useful place to refuel with competent modern European cooking. ££

The Rose Tea Shop
51 High Street; tel: 01865 244 429; http://the-rose.biz/home.htm; Tue–Sat 9am–6pm, Sun 10am–6pm. This homely café sits towards the western end of the High Street and serves breakfast, lunch and afternoon tea. The selection of teas is bewildering and the service is friendly. £

Tour 5

The High Street

This is not your usual high street experience; at a little over a mile (1.6 km), this morning or afternoon's stroll will take in some of the grandest colleges and some unusual shops

The High Street (or 'the High' as it is known locally) is different from other streets in central Oxford in that it is curved rather than straight. This is because the grid layout of the original Saxon town was out of alignment with the crossing point of the River Cherwell to the east, where Magdalen Bridge now stands. In times gone by, as you left the town by its original east gate, the road became nothing more than a track, and curved gently down to the river. Over the centuries, not only colleges but also inns and shops were built alongside, endowing the curve with the grace and elegance we see today and inspiring Nikolaus Pevsner to describe the High as 'one of the world's greatest streets'.

Highlights

- The shops on the High Street
- Shelley Memorial, University College
- The Queen's College
- Magdalen College
- Addison's Walk and deer park
- Punting from Magdalen Bridge

TRAFFIC CALMING

Historically, the High Street has always been busy. In the 18th and 19th centuries, the coach-and-four to London departed with ever increasing rapidity from inns such as The Angel and The Mitre. Traffic congestion in the 20th century led to several attempts to limit the numbers of vehicles, including a (thankfully abandoned) scheme to construct a link road from St Ebbe's church across Christ Church Meadow, following the line of the Broad Walk (see p.51). In 1999 the street was finally closed to general traffic – buses excepted – during the daytime.

HISTORIC FACADES

The **Carfax ❶** end of the High Street (see p.41) is the commercial end, mostly taken up by shops and the odd restaurant, as well as the long facade of the **Covered Market ❷** (see p.40). But there are interesting details that are worth examining. Starting on the south side, take a look at the sign above the silversmith's at **No. 131**: a white dog with a giant watch in its mouth. Just here, a small alley – one of many that delineated the original medieval plots along this part of the street – leads down to the **Chequers Inn ❸**, a 15th-century tavern.

The next alley along is signposted to the Chiang Mai Kitchen (see Eating Out, p.65), a Thai restaurant housed in the venerable **Kemp Hall**. Built by an alderman in 1637, this is a fine example of the many timber-framed houses that sprang up all over Oxford

Left: view of 'the High' from Carfax Tower. **Above**: Carfax Tower presides over one end of the High Street.

during the great rebuilding of the city during the 16th and 17th centuries. The old wooden door with its projecting canopy is original, as are many of the windows; the interior is also very well preserved.

Back on the High Street, the next building of interest on this side is to be

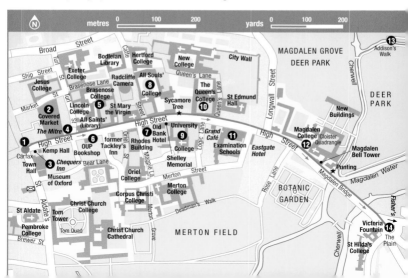

Above: Oxford University Press Bookshop at Nos 116–17 on the High.

found at **No. 126**. With its elegantly curved windows and fine proportions, this is the best-preserved example of a 17th-century facade in Oxford. But the building itself actually dates back a lot further than this, for it is known to have been owned by a bell founder before being taken over by St Frideswide's Abbey in 1350. This is the story of many of the buildings along the High Street – they are medieval in origin but were given new facades later.

ANCIENT INN

Cross the road at the traffic lights to arrive at **The Mitre ❹**, now housing a chain pub-restaurant, but once a popular student inn. It was built in about 1600 over a 13th-century vault, which sadly can no longer be visited. Nevertheless, The Mitre remains full of history, enlivened by anecdotes of ale-supping clergy. A sign in the lobby recalls its role as a coaching inn.

The Mitre stands on the corner of Turl Street (see p.37), and on the opposite corner stands the **former All Saints' Church**, now used as a library by Lincoln College. Beyond this is the High Street frontage of **Brasenose College ❺** (see p.20), which despite looking positively medieval was only built in the latter part of the 19th and early 20th centuries.

Ⓢ Butcher, Baker and Candlestick Maker...

Unlike many British high streets, the High has retained much of its historical character. This is in large part owing to the variety of its shops and the virtual absence of the large chain stores. Working from west to east, the most interesting shops include Ede and Ravescroft (tailor's) at No. 119, Sanders (fine prints and pictures) at No. 104, Brora (womens' cashmere clothing) at No. 102, Pod (inspiring gifts) at Nos 86–7, Reginald Davis (silversmith and jeweller) at No. 34, Waterfield's (second-hand books) at No. 52, Antiques on High at No. 85, Hoyles Games and Puzzles at No. 72 and Plus Pens (fine stationery) at Nos 69–70.

Above: the High is lined with quirky shops housed in beautiful buildings.

OXFORD UNIVERSITY PRESS BOOKSHOP

On the south side is a fine run of buildings with 18th-century facades. Nos 117–118 have a fine Art Nouveau shop window, while next door at Nos 116–17 are the premises of the **Oxford University Press Bookshop** ❻ (Mon–Sat 9am–5.30pm, Wed from 9.30am, Sun 11am–5pm), which sells only the books that the Press publishes. Further down, beyond King Edward Street, **Nos 106 and 107** (University of Oxford Shop and A-Plan Insurance) are particularly interesting. Together they were originally Tackley's Inn, built in 1320 and subsequently rented out as an academic hall. A-Plan may allow you through to the back of their premises to see the 16th-century roof structure of the Hall as well as a large medieval window. The cellar is considered the best medieval cellar in Oxford.

On the other side of Oriel Street, opposite the church of **St Mary the Virgin** (see p.21), stands the **Rhodes Building** of Oriel College, built in 1910 from funds bequeathed by Cecil

Ⓕ Screams in the Night

The Mitre Inn was the scene of one of the worst chapters in the city's long history of religious intolerance. During Henry VIII's Dissolution of the Monasteries, a secret tunnel linked The Mitre with buildings across the High Street. It seems that Henry's soldiers drove a group of monks underground and then bricked up both ends of the tunnel. It is said that the monks' screams can still be heard today in the dead of night.

Above: The Mitre is full of ale and history.

Rhodes, who, after completing his education at Oriel made a fortune in Southern Africa and ultimately gave his name to Rhodesia (now Zimbabwe). Rhodes also endowed Rhodes Scholarships at Oxford, one of the most notable beneficiaries being Bill Clinton.

UNIVERSITY COLLEGE

Continue along the south side, crossing Magpie Lane and passing by the **Old Bank Hotel** ❼ with its smart restaurant, the Quod Restaurant and Bar (see p.23). On the opposite side of the road is the High Street range of **All Souls' College** ❽ (see p.20).

Above: stained-glass window of Athelstan, King of England from 924 to 939, in the chapel of All Souls' College.

Above: University College is another fine example of the now familiar Oxford Jacobean-Gothic style.

Dating from the 14th and 15th centuries, this is the oldest surviving part of the college; it was, however, refaced in the 19th century. A line of grotesque sculptures runs beneath the parapet.

Continuing on the south side, we now come to the long frontage of **University College 9** (tel: 01865 276 602; www.univ.ox.ac.uk; enquire at the porter's lodge for permission to enter). Claiming to be the oldest

college in Oxford, 'Univ' is thought to have been founded in 1249 with funds left by William of Durham, who had fled from Paris after a row between the kings of France and England. None of the original buildings remain, however, and the college you see today was built with substantial benefactions in the 17th century. The range facing the High is in two parts, firstly the front quad (with main entrance),

F Shelley Memorial

Before reaching the main range of University College, you may have noticed a small dome peeping above the wall. This covers the monument to Percy Bysshe Shelley, who was expelled after only six months at the college, in 1811, for circulating a pamphlet, *The Necessity of Atheism*. The monument, depicting the naked body of the poet, who was drowned off Livorno in 1822, can be reached via a passageway in the northwest corner of the front quad (assuming the porter lets you in).

Above: the poet is supported by winged lions and the Muse of Poetry.

Above: the beautiful carved entrance to University College.

completed in the 1670s, and beyond that the Radcliffe Quad, almost an exact copy completed 40 years later. The gate-towers contain, respectively, the statues of Queen Anne and Queen Mary. On the inner face of the front quad is a **statue of James II**, wearing a toga. This is one of only two statues in England of this most unpopular Catholic king.

If you do manage to get into the college, make a point of visiting the chapel. Although refurbished by Sir George Gilbert Scott in 1862, it still retains its original, finely detailed stained glass, designed by the German artist Abraham von Linge.

THE QUEEN'S COLLEGE

As well as in Lincoln College (see p.39) and University College, further examples of Linge's stained glass can be admired in the chapel of **The Queen's College** ❿ (tel: 01865 279 120; www.queens.ox.ac.uk; access only with an official guided tour booked at the Tourist Information Centre, see p.124). The college is named after Queen Philippa, wife of Edward

II, whose chaplain, Robert Eglesfeld, founded it in 1340. The statue under the little dome above the gate-house, however, is that of Queen Caroline, who donated substantial funds to the rebuilding of Queen's in the 18th century. The college's magnificent Baroque screen now dominates the northern side of the High Street. Inside, the chapel occupies the right hand side of the front quad's north range, while the left side is given over to the Hall, scene every December of the famous Boar's Head Feast; this commemorates a Queen's student who is said to have killed a wild boar by ramming a copy of Aristotle's works down its throat.

SYCAMORE TREE

To the left of Queen's and directly opposite the gatehouse of University College's front quad stands a lone **sycamore tree**, whose presence endows the High Street with a rural flavour. As the only landmark that can be seen from both ends, it has long been regarded as Oxford's most significant tree and has even

Above: Queen Caroline occupies pride of place under her dome in The Queen's College.

Above: the stately colonnaded New Buildings were intended to be part of a huge neoclassical quadrangle but funds ran out and only one range was built.

been described as one of the most important trees in Europe.

Continue along the south side of the High Street, passing the Grand Café *(see Eating Out, p.65)* at No. 84, with its elegant windows and Corinthian columns. Until the mid-19th century, this was part of the historic Angel Inn, one of Oxford's most important coaching inns (in 1831 it was operating no less than 11 daily coach services to London and 13 others to various parts of the country). The premises, together with No. 83 next door, then became a grocery shop belonging to Frank Cooper *(see box opposite)*. No. 83 now houses offices of the Oxford Bus Company; note the delightful first-floor Venetian window.

EXAMINATION SCHOOLS

Next along is the massive block of the **Examination Schools ⓫**, built in 1882 on the site of the Angel Inn. Introduced only in the late 18th century, the first written exams were held in the Divinity School, before moving to various rooms in the Old Schools Quadrangle. By the second half of the

19th century, however, a new, purpose-built edifice was required.

The building was designed by T.G. Jackson in the style of a Jacobean country house, with Classical and Gothic elements, and the result, especially the High Street facade, has sometimes been described as heavy-handed – designed, perhaps, to intimidate the hapless exam candidates.

Above: the gate of the massive Examination Schools, the students' least favourite building.

charge) was founded in 1458 by William Waynflete, Bishop of Winchester and Lord Chancellor of England under King Henry VI. It was built on the site of the Hospital of St John the Baptist, some of whose buildings survive as part of the college's High Street range. Built outside the city walls, Magdalen had lots of space in which to expand, and its grounds encompass large areas of meadow, bounded in the east by the River Cherwell.

The Bell Tower

Completed in 1505, the **Bell Tower** is famous for the Latin grace sung from the top by the choristers every May Morning. The tradition probably dates back to the tower's inauguration, but there were no loudspeakers in those

Students can be seen entering and leaving the building in the exam months of May and June, all dressed in 'subfusc' garb without which they are not allowed to sit their exam. For men, this means dark suit and white bow tie; for women, it is a black skirt or trousers, white blouse and a black ribbon round the neck. All must also wear a black academic gown and a mortar board.

On the same corner stands the **Eastgate Hotel** *(see p.53)*. It was at this point that the east gate through the medieval town wall stood until its demolition at the hands of the Paving Commission in 1772. There has been an inn on this site since 1605, but the present hotel was built in 1899 in the style of a 17th-century town house.

Continue as far as the Longwall Street traffic lights, where you cross on to the north side of the road and proceed towards Magdalen College, the famous tower of which dominates the eastern end of the High Street.

MAGDALEN COLLEGE

Magdalen College ⑫ (pronounced 'maudlin'; tel: 01865 276 000; www.magd.ox.ac.uk; Oct–June 1–7pm or dusk if earlier, July–Sept noon–6pm;

🅕 Frank Cooper

It was at No. 84 High Street, in 1874, that Frank Cooper began selling jars of surplus marmalade produced by his wife, Sarah Jane, from an old family recipe on her kitchen range. It proved so popular that a specially designed factory was constructed on Park End Street. Although the firm sold out in 1974, the marmalade is still manufactured under the original label and sold all over the world.

Above: Frank Cooper's marmalade remains a breakfast favourite.

Above: the Bell Tower at Magdalen College, completed in 1505.

Dancers and students take their lovers off by punt for champagne breakfasts along the banks of the River Cherwell.

During the Civil War, the tower was used as a vantage point by the Royalist forces who had established themselves in the city after the Battle of Edgehill in 1642. But while Magdalen, along with the rest of the university, lent its full support to Charles I, it did not support the unpopular James II, who attempted to make the college a Catholic seminary.

In 1687, James had his own man (Bishop Parker) installed briefly as college President and had Mass run by Jesuit appointees, set up in the chapel. With the advance of the Protestant William of Orange, however, James promptly did a U-turn and had the original Fellows reinstated on 25 October 1688, an event still celebrated in Magdalen as Restoration Day. But it was too late for the unfortunate king, who soon lost his crown and spent the rest of his life in exile in France.

days, and, one assumes, the crowds at the bottom were considerably smaller. When the singing finishes the bells ring out, sparking off a whole morning of revelries, including performances in the town by the Headington Morris

Above: the picturesque tree-lined Addison's Walk.

G Deer Spotting

Deer have occupied the grounds of Magdalen College ever since the early 18th century, when they were introduced in order to supply the college with venison. They can be seen grazing either in Magdalen Grove behind the New Buildings or on the meadows adjacent to the Cherwell (visible from Addison's Walk). They are usually moved to the latter in May, when the fritillary blossoms are over.

Above: deer happily grazing in Magdalen Grove.

A series of quadrangles

Entering the college via the porter's lodge on the High Street, take the diagonal path across **St John's Quadrangle**. To the right of the Founder's Tower, a vaulted passageway provides access to the **chapel** through a doorway on the right. Originally built in 1480, the chapel was completely redesigned in the early 18th century. But with its

stone vaulting and ornamental screens, it is still worth seeing, its most interesting feature being the sepia stained-glass windows in the ante-chapel.

Returning to the passageway outside, continue to the end and you emerge into the lovely **Cloister Quadrangle**, the 15th-century core of the college. With its vaulted walkways, the quad still looks authentically ancient, even though the north and east wings had to be rebuilt in the early 19th century after attempts were made to have the Cloisters cleared to make way for the New Buildings. Completed in 1733, the **New Buildings** were intended to be part of a huge neoclassical quadrangle. Fortunately, the money ran out and only one range was ever built. It stands alone at the back of the college, reached by exiting the Cloister Quadrangle via the tunnel on the north side.

Opposite the New Buildings, walk along the path to the left (west) to see the massive plane tree, planted in 1801; it is a descendant of a hybrid developed by Jacob Bobart in the Botanic Garden on the other side of the High Street.

Addison's Walk

In the other direction (east), cross the bridge over an arm of the Cherwell to follow **Addison's Walk** ⓑ, a delightful tree-lined path that runs along a raised causeway that was partly created out of the remains of Charles I's Civil War defences. The path follows a circular route of about a mile around the Cherwell's water meadows. It is named after Joseph Addison (1672–1719), poet and Spectator essayist, whose rooms in Magdalen College overlooked these meadows. At the far northeast corner of the walk, a wooden bridge over the Cherwell provides access to Magdalen's **Fellows' Garden** (private), the extensive lawns of which emphasise just how much space the college has at its disposal.

The meadows and the riverbanks support an abundance of flora, including the rare purple and white snake's head fritillary, which blooms in the spring and grows wild in only a few places in Britain. But both the meadow and the groves of Addison's Walk are a delight at any time of year; on summer weekends, the Cherwell is busy with the traffic of punters who embark and alight at Magdalen Bridge.

Above: rowing boats moored under Magdalen Bridge.

Now return to the entrance of the college via the cloisters and then the Chaplain's Quadrangle. To the left, the Bell Tower soars heavenwards and to its right is the oldest part of the college – a section of the 13th-century hospital incorporated into the High Street range. Passing from the Chaplain's Quadrangle into St John's Quadrangle, you will notice on the left wall an outside pulpit, from where a service is conducted once a year on the Feast of St John the Baptist (June 24), a tradition that dates back to the earliest days of the college.

MAGDALEN BRIDGE

As you exit Magdalen, you will notice on the opposite side of the street the main entrance to the Botanic Garden (see p.52), incorporating the fine archway paid for by the founder, the Earl of Danby. Set into the arch is his statue, as well as that of Charles II in the niche to the right and that of Charles I on the left.

Continuing, however, along the north side, you walk past Magdalen's High Street range with its impressive array of gargoyles. Just beyond, some steps lead down to a landing stage, the main one in the city for visitors wishing to try their hand at **punting** (see p.44).

The first bridge built across the Cherwell at this point was a timber construction erected in 1004. It was replaced by a stone-built structure in the 16th century, but this was demolished during the Civil War in the 1640s and replaced with a drawbridge. The present **Magdalen Bridge** dates from 1772. It has since been widened a couple of times to cope with the ever-increasing volume of traffic.

On the other side you'll find **The Plain** ⓮, the busy traffic junction of St Clements, Cowley and Iffley roads. In the middle stands the **Victoria**

Above: Fisher's opened in 1995 to great reviews and featured in *The Times*' top 10 Best Fish Restaurants in the UK.

Fountain, which was donated by the Morrells Brewery in 1899 and used as a drinking trough for horses. Until its destruction at the hands of the Paving Commission in 1772, the church of St Clements had stood on this site. The fine 18th-century house on the right is occupied by **St Hilda's College** (tel: 01865 276 884; www.st-hildas.ox.ac.uk; by appointment only), which until 2008 was the last remaining college for women only in Oxford. Its grounds enjoy remarkable views of the Cherwell and Christ Church Meadow.

E Eating Out

The Chequers
131a High Street; tel: 01865 727 463; Mon–Sat 11am–11.30pm, Sun 11am–10.30pm, food served 10am–10pm. Well-maintained 15th-century inn hidden down an alleyway off the High Street. Popular with a non-student clientele, it has a pleasant courtyard area. Serves a full English at breakfast and simple pub grub for lunch. £

Chiang Mai Kitchen
130a High Street; tel: 01865 202 233; www.chiangmaikitchen.co.uk; daily lunch and dinner.
Stylish and authentic Thai cuisine served in a beautifully preserved Tudor building. Extensive vegetarian options are on offer, and the staff are very helpful with queries. ££

Fisher's
36–7 St Clements; tel: 01865 243 003; www.fishers-restaurant.com. Although Oxford is just about as far as you can get from the coast in Britain, this restaurant specialises in fresh fish and seafood. Look out for the good-value set-lunch menus. ££–£££

Grand Café
84 High Street; tel: 01865 204 463; www.thegrandcafe.co.uk; café: daily 9am–7pm, bar: Mon–Sat 7–11pm.
Housed in the old marmalade factory – a throw-back to Edwardian grandeur – this establishment operates as a smart café by day (breakfasts, light meals and afternoon teas), and a chic cocktail bar by night. £–££

Tour 6

From Carfax to the River

This full-day, one-mile tour explores the worlds of *Alice in Wonderland* and *Harry Potter*, while taking in art galleries, Oxford's cathedral and rowing on the river

Top: Salters Steamers near Folly Bridge. **Above**: happy faces inside Modern Art Oxford.

Highlights

- Museum of Oxford
- Modern Art Oxford
- Christ Church college and Cathedral
- Bate Collection of Musical Instruments
- Boat races on the river in season

The road heading south from Carfax is St Aldate's. It was here, down the hill towards the River Thames, that the first Oxford settlement is thought to have been established, beside the Abbey of St Frideswide. St Frideswide's later formed the core of the huge complex that is Christ Church. This is now perhaps Oxford's most famous college, renowned as much for its associations with Lewis Carroll, *Brideshead Revisited* and *Harry Potter* as for the beauty of its historic fabric.

OXFORD TOWN HALL AND MUSEUM

From Carfax, walk down the left-hand side of St Aldate's. The stone building just on the left is the **Town Hall ①**. Opened in 1897, this fine neo-Jacobean edifice was built to the greater glory of the City Council, reflecting Oxford's new-found status and self-confidence after it was declared a county borough in 1889. Above, the three-tiered belvedere on the roof is topped by a weathervane in the shape of a horned ox – for Oxford was originally called Oxenford. The Town Hall once contained the city archives; these are now housed in the County Hall.

Just around the corner, in Blue Boar Street, is the entrance to the former city library, built at the same time as the Town Hall and now housing the **Museum of Oxford ②** (tel: 01865 252 761; www.museumofoxford.org. uk; Mon–Sat 10am–5pm, Sun 11am–3pm; charge). Displays inside highlight the history of the city from prehistoric times to the industrial age. There are reconstructions of Roman kilns found at Headington, exhibits from the Abbey of St Frideswide, documents on the origins of the university and photographs showing the development of car manufacturing at Cowley. The most macabre exhibit is the skeleton of Giles Covington, an Oxford Freeman who was convicted of murder and executed in 1791 *(see box right)*. There is also a display featuring some of the belongings of Alice Liddell, including her parasol, and the morning dress she would have worn on outings with Charles Dodgson (aka Lewis Carroll). *Alice in Wonderland* activity packs are available for children.

⑥ Royal Pardon?

Giles Covington went to the gallows in 1791 protesting his innocence. The 23-year-old seaman had been convicted of the murder four years previously of David Charteris, a Scottish pedlar, near Abingdon. Among the prime suspects was Richard Kilby, an army deserter, who was arrested but offered to turn King's Evidence in return for a Royal Pardon. It was he who pointed the finger at Covington. There has been a campaign – sadly unsuccessful – to have the case re-examined, in the hope of obtaining a Royal Pardon for Covington, as well as a proper burial. Having first done time as a teaching aide in an anatomy school, the exhibit the University Museum once labelled simply 'Englishman' is yet to rest in peace.

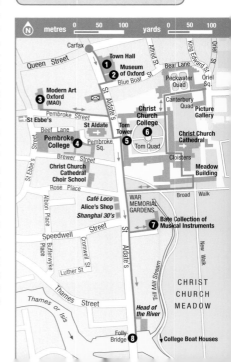

MUSEUM OF MODERN ART

At this point, fans of modern art should cross St Aldate's and, after the post office, turn right into peaceful Pembroke Street. At the very end on the right is **Modern Art Oxford** ❸ (tel: 01865 722 733; www.modernartoxford.org.uk; Tue–Wed 10am–5pm, Thur–Sat 10am–7pm, Sun noon–5pm; free), which occupies an old brewery warehouse and mounts important exhibitions of contemporary art. The gallery also runs lots of activities for children, including 'The Modern Art Trolley' from 2–4pm on weekend afternoons (no need to book – just drop in). The gallery café is also worth mentioning – and is a good place to rest the legs.

Outside again, the church on the corner on St Ebbe's Street is St Ebbe's, dedicated to a 12th-century Northumbrian abbess. The only truly ancient part of the building is the 12th-century doorway; the rest was rebuilt in 1816.

PEMBROKE COLLEGE

Return now to St Aldate's, where the eponymous evangelical church stands back from the main road in leafy Pembroke Square. The square also provides access, on its south side, to **Pembroke College** ❹ (tel: 01865 276 444; www.pmb.ox.ac.uk; enquire at the porter's lodge for access; free). The college was founded in 1624 by King James I, and his statue occupies a niche in the tower of the Hall, built in 1848 but looking convincingly 15th-century. The Renaissance-style chapel (1732) has a fine painted ceiling, as well as stained glass completed in 1900 by Charles Kempe, a former student. Another former student was the lexicographer Dr Samuel Johnson, who never completed his degree here but was awarded an honorary degree by the university in recognition of his achievements in compiling the first English dictionary.

Above: colourful art installation inside Modern Art Oxford.

Osney Abbey to the west of the town (see p.81), which was completely destroyed at the Dissolution in 1536. The bell is named not after Thomas Wolsey, the founder of Christ Church, but after Thomas Becket, the archbishop of Canterbury brutally murdered by King Henry II's henchmen in 1170.

Just to the north of the tower are the rooms where Charles Dodgson, alias Lewis Carroll, author of *Alice's Adventures in Wonderland*, last resided while at Christ Church. Dodgson, a mathematics don at the college, made friends with Alice, the daughter of the Dean, while taking photographs of the cathedral from the deanery garden, and together they plunged into their own fantasy world (see box below).

Above: Christopher Wren's Tom Tower.

THE TOM TOWER

On the opposite side of the street from Pembroke Square looms the magnificent **Tom Tower** ❺, built over the entrance to Christ Church by Christopher Wren in 1681. Inside, the Great Tom bell chimes 101 times each evening (once for each member of the original foundation) at 9.05pm, Oxford being situated a stubborn five minutes west of Greenwich. Recast before being installed in the tower, the original bell came from the enormous

CHRIST CHURCH

Because there is usually no public access to Christ Church through the entrance under the Tom Tower, continue down the right-hand side of St Aldate's to arrive at **Alice's Shop** (see below).

Directly opposite of is a fine view of Christ Church and the cathedral rising beyond the War Memorial Gardens. The gardens provide access to the college's public entrance, through the **Meadow Building**.

ⓢ Alice's Shop

On the opposite side of St Aldate's from Tom Tower and a little further down is **Alice's Shop** (tel: 01865 723 793; www.aliceinwonderlandshop. co.uk). In *Through the Looking Glass* Alice visits the shop and is served by a bad-tempered sheep, and it was drawn in the book by Sir John Tenniel as as 'the Old Sheep Shop'. Alice herself described it as 'the very queerest shop I ever saw!' Today, the shop is devoted to the sale of souvenirs related to the Lewis Carroll stories.

Above: where Alice Liddell bought her barley sugar before setting out on river trips with Charles Dodgson.

Above: Christ Church seen from across the Trill Mill Stream.

Christ Church ❻ (tel: 01865 276 492; www.chch.ox.ac.uk; college and cathedral: Mon–Sat 9am–5pm, Sun 2–5pm; guided tours available; charge) was founded as Cardinal College in 1525 by Thomas Wolsey, Henry VIII's all-powerful Lord Chancellor. The college was built on the site of a priory thought to have been founded by St Frideswide, as long ago as AD730 *(see box opposite)* – and indeed the earliest Oxford settlement may have been a lay community serving St Frideswide's (Saxon tools, artefacts and items of clothing have been found during excavations in St Aldate's). The first documentary evidence for the town, however, comes in a royal charter of King Ethelred the Unready, compensating the community for the burning down of its church by the Danes in 1002. The priory was refounded by the Augustinians in the 12th century, and by the time Wolsey came along it had become an extensive abbey. Wolsey dissolved it, and took the endowments to found his new college.

But his grand scheme came to an end in 1529, when he fell from grace after failing to secure the speedy an-nulment of Henry VIII's marriage to Catherine of Aragon. Henry rescued the church and took over the college, refounding it as King Henry VIII's College in 1532. Ten years later, Oxford was made a diocese and the priory elevated to the status of cathedral, which Henry then combined with the college and renaming it Christ Church in 1546. The church is thus unique in being both a college chapel and a cathedral.

Above: the Cloisters.

The cloisters

Having entered Christ Church, continue through to the **cloisters**, which date from the 15th century. Wolsey destroyed the west and south sides of the cloisters, as well as three bays of the priory church, to make way for Tom Quad. Through the first doorway on the right, the 13th-century Old Chapter House now houses a souvenir shop as well as a collection of cathedral and college treasures.

The Cathedral

Enter the Cathedral via the next door on the right. Much of the old priory church part of the Cathedral is rather disappointing from an architectural point of view. The aisles are too squat when compared to the size of the columns, and the small pairs of rounded arches fit too awkwardly into the main ones. By contrast, the 15th-century choir with its lierne-vaulted ceiling is truly magnificent.

Just to the north of the choir is the **shrine of St Frideswide**. The original shrine dated back to 1289, but was destroyed during the Reformation. What you see today is the result of reconstruction in 1889. The intri-

cately carved canopy has faces peering through sculpted leaves of ivy and sycamore, oak and vine — a medieval mason's interpretation of the virgin princess's escape from her persistent suitor, Algar, to the safety of the forest. The body of the saint is no longer in the tomb itself; after the destruction of the shrine it was reburied beneath a nearby gravestone.

The life of the saint is depicted in stained glass in the adjacent **Latin Chapel**. Designed in 1858 by Edward Burne-Jones, the dramatic scenes include a depiction of St Margaret's Well at Binsey (the 'Treacle Well' from *Alice's Adventures in Wonderland* – see p.105). In 1877, Burne-Jones also designed the St Catherine Window in the chapel to

⑤ St Frideswide

Legend has it that the Saxon priory on which Christ Church now stands was built by Frideswide, a Mercian princess, as a means to preserve her virginity. When a persistent suitor tried to take Frideswide by force, he was struck blind; only when the saintly Frideswide forgave him was his sight restored. Frideswide was buried in her monastery, which became the nucleus of the nascent town of Oxford, and she is now the city's patron saint.

Above: St Frideswide's stained-glass detail inside the Latin Chapel.

Above: Christ Church Hall will be familiar to the millions who have enjoyed the film versions of the *Harry Potter* novels.

the south of the choir, depicting Edith Liddell, sister of Lewis Carroll's Alice, as the saint. The glass was made by William Morris; other works by these two Pre-Raphaelite artists are dotted throughout the Cathedral.

The Hall

Exiting the Cathedral by the same door by which you entered, follow the cloisters round to the left, arriving, just before the opening to the Tom Quad, at the foot of the staircase to **the Hall**. Designed by James Wyatt in 1829, the stairs were built under the splendid fan-vaulted ceiling, which had been created almost 200 years earlier, in 1640, by Dean Samuel Fell. The best view of the ceiling, and the single slender pillar supporting it, is from the top of the stairs.

Across the landing is the entrance to the Hall. With its magnificent hammerbeam roof, this is easily the largest old hall in Oxford, representing the full splendour of the Tudor court. The room proved a convincing stand-in for Hogwarts Hall in the *Harry Potter* films. Around its walls are hung portraits of some of the college's alumni, including William Gladstone and Anthony Eden (two of the 13 prime ministers produced by Christ Church) as well as John Locke, the great philosopher, and William Penn, the founder of Pennsylvania. Above the High Table is a portrait of the college's second founder, Henry VIII. The portrait just inside the door is that of Charles Dodgson.

Above: Christ Church custodian.

Tom Quad

Exit the Hall and enter the vast **Tom Quad**. Measuring 264ft by 261ft (80m by 79m), this is by far the largest quadrangle in the city. The whole of the south side, including the Hall and kitchens, and most of the east and west sides, were completed before the demise of Wolsey, who intended the entire quad to be cloistered (as can be seen from the arches in the stonework); the north range was completed 130 years later. In the central pond is a statue of Mercury, which was erected in 1928 to replace the one damaged by a student (the later Earl of Derby) in 1817. Beyond is the distinctive form of the Tom Tower (see p.69).

Quad to quad

Follow the eastern range of the quad to the northeastern corner where the **Deanery**, with its castellated parapet, faces onto the quad. It was here, during the Civil War, that Charles I resided. The south facade is embellished with a statue of the autocratic Dean John Fell, son of the Samuel Fell who designed the ceiling above the steps to the Hall. The Deanery Garden is just over the other side.

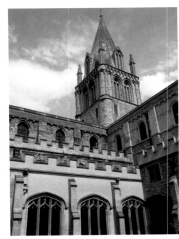

Above: The Cathedral was begun when Norman architecture was giving way to the Early English Style.

Pass through the archway and enter the neoclassical **Peckwater Quad**, built in 1713 on the site of a medieval inn. The three enclosed sides of the quad are perfectly proportioned, in accordance with all the classical rules. Opposite stands the college **Library** (closed to the public), built in 1716 and originally designed with the ground

The Isis

The stretch of the Thames between Folly Bridge and Iffley Lock is popularly known as The Isis. It is here that the college rowing crews race against each other in the two annual regattas – 'Torpids' in late-February and 'Eights' in mid-May. Iffley Lock is about 1½ miles (2.5km) from Folly Bridge, and you can get to it by crossing the bridge and following the path along the south bank. There is a pub called the Isis Tavern, and, if you have time, you can cross the lock and visit the Romanesque church of St Mary the Virgin.

Above: the bucolic setting of Iffley Lock.

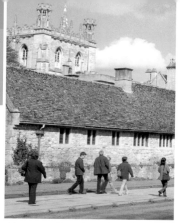

Above: strolling along the college's extensive grounds.

floor as an open loggia. Its Corinthian columns lend weight and splendour to this side of the quadrangle.

From Peckwater Quad, proceed to **Canterbury Quad**. On the right is the **Picture Gallery** (tel: 01865 276 172; Jun–Sept Mon–Sat 10.30am–5pm, Sun 2–5pm, Oct–May Mon–Sat 10.30am–1pm, 2–4.30pm, Sun 2–4.30pm; Oct–Jun closed Tue; charge), which contains a small but important collection of Old Masters, including works by Tintoretto, Veronese and Van Dyck, as well as a famous

Holbein portrait of Henry VIII. Visitors are obliged to leave the college via the Canterbury Quad exit, into Merton Lane and Oriel Square (see p.46).

BATE COLLECTION

Because of the way the official route round Christ Church is organised – starting at the Meadow Building and finishing in Merton Lane – visitors may wish, before entering, to continue down St Aldate's towards the River Thames.

On the left-hand side of the road, a gateway leads to the University Music Faculty and the **Bate Collection of Musical Instruments ❼** (tel: 01865 276 139; www.bate.ox.ac.uk; Mon–Fri 2–5pm, also Sat 10am–noon during term time; guided tours by arrangement; charge). Established in 1963 from a donation by a private collector, Philip Bate, the collection represents an unrivalled survey of European woodwind instruments, since added to by numerous donations of brass instruments, pianos, clavichords and harpsichords, as well as a fine gamelan from Indonesia. Check out the website for fun family events, including opportunities to try out some of the instruments in the collection.

FOLLY BRIDGE

Further down St Aldate's, with the redeveloped district of St Ebbe's on the right, lies **Folly Bridge ❽**. This is thought to be the site of the first crossing point or 'oxen-ford' over the Thames, created in the 8th century to serve the expanding Saxon community. Remains of a more substantial causeway (Grandpont), built here by the town's Norman governor, Robert d'Oilly, can be seen if you pass under the bridge in a boat. The present bridge dates from 1827.

From Folly Bridge, visitors can enter through the turnstile gate lo-

Above: the Bate Collection's gamelan, a musical ensemble from Indonesia featuring a variety of instruments.

Above: boats moored near Folly Bridge.

cated behind the **Head of the River pub** (see *Eating Out, below*) and walk along the Thames to the college boat houses. During the Trinity (summer) term in May, this is the scene of Eights Week (see p.45). Apart from watching the boats, the walk along the river here is very pleasant. Just before the boat houses, near the small bridge at the confluence of the Cherwell and the Thames, the views across Christ Church Meadow, with the spires of Oxford in the background, are magnificent. From here, you can also follow the Cherwell back to Broad Walk, or alternatively walk directly to Christ Church along New Walk (see also p.51).

Ⓔ Eating Out

Café Loco
The Old Palace, 85–7 St Aldate's, tel: 01865 200 959; www.goingloco. com; daily breakfast, lunch and afternoon tea.
Located within a 16th-century bishop's palace, this beautiful café serves high-quality food at very reasonable prices. £

Head of the River
Folly Bridge, St Aldate's; tel: 01865 721 600; www.headoftheriveroxford. co.uk; daily noon–11pm, food served until 9pm.
This grand old inn on the banks of the river is always a convivial place to be, but is especially so in the summer, when the crowds spill out on to the extensive terrace. What's more, the beer is good and the food – traditional British in style – is hearty and filling. ££

Modern Art Oxford Café
30 Pembroke Street; tel: 01865 813 814; Tue–Sat 10am–5pm, Sun noon–5pm.
Pleasant café serving simple lunches (with ingredients bought from the Covered Market) and providing excellent facilities for adults (wi-fi access) and children (kids' menus, high chairs and changing facilities) alike. £

Shanghai 30's
82 St Aldate's; tel: 01865 242 230; www.shanghai30s.com; Tue–Sun lunch and dinner, Mon dinner only.
Set in a wooden-pannelled first-floor room overlooking St Aldate's, this Chinese restaurant aims to recapture something of the luxury that could have been experienced in Shanghai in the 1930s. The food certainly lives up to this ambition, with fresh flavours and extravagant presentation. £££

Tour 7

West of the City Centre

This half-day tour includes a mile-long walk around an area that at one time was dominated by a Norman castle, and then much later by the brewing industry

From medieval times onwards, the western part of the city, centred on the Castle Mill Stream, was crowded with wharves unloading cargo from the upper Thames. As the Industrial Revolution got under way, the city was linked with the Midlands by canal (in 1790), and the area became a bustling inland port. Activity declined with the arrival of the railway in 1844, though the brewing industry managed to continue production here until 1999.

BONN SQUARE

From **Carfax ❶** (see p.41) walk along Queen Street, which is lined with chain stores and is every bit as busy as Cornmarket Street, but with the addition of buses nudging nose to tail through the crowds of shoppers. In

the summer, some light relief is provided by **Bonn Square ❷**, named after Oxford's twin city in Germany, and a popular meeting place, with buskers often performing. On the opposite side of the road you'll see the ugly concrete **Westgate Shopping Centre**, slated for a massive redevelopment that at the time of writing has yet to begin, but is optimistically scheduled for completion in 2014.

Left: your guides at Oxford Castle Unlocked. **Above**: Nuffield College Tower; you either love it or hate it.

NUFFIELD COLLEGE

Continue downhill on to New Road, the construction of which across the castle bailey in 1769 marked the beginning of local road improvements. Such developments were then formalised by the creation of the Paving Commission two years later (see p.40). On the left you will see the fortress-like facade of County Hall, the headquarters of Oxfordshire County Council, while down the hill on the right is the unmistakable spire of **Nuffield College** ❸ (tel: 01865 278 500; www.nuffield. ox.ac.uk; enquire at the porter's lodge for access; free).

The site and funds for the college were donated to the university in 1937 by Lord Nuffield, otherwise known as William Richard Morris, who began life repairing bicycles in the High Street, progressed to designing the 'Bullnose' Morris in Longwall Street (see p.31) and ended up by establishing the first ever mass-production line for cheap cars out at Cowley. His manufacturing goals achieved, Nuffield used part of

ⓢ Shopping Spree

Among the more interesting shops you will encounter along this route are Arcadia (gifts and Victorian prints) at Nos 2–4 St Michael's Street, Tiger-lily (alternative fashion plus piercing and tattooing) at Nos 3–7 New Inn Hall Street, Scribbler (smart stationery) at Nos 6–8 New Inn Hall Street, and Games Workshop (toys and models) on the corner of New Inn Hall Street and George Street.

Above: more high-brow shopping.

his vast fortune for good causes, including hospitals and charities. As far as the university was concerned, he had originally envisaged establishing a college specialising in engineering, but was persuaded instead to fund a post-graduate college devoted to the study of social, economic and political problems.

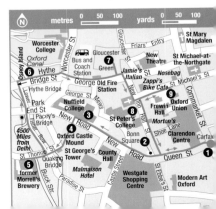

Above: prepare for some gruesome tales at Oxford Castle Unlocked.

Attractive to some, plain ugly to others, the Stalinesque-style tower houses the college library. Only completed in 1960, the rest of the college is much like a Cotswold country house, with buildings grouped around two attractive courtyards in the pattern of traditional colleges.

Above: behind the gate, the forbidding-looking Debtors' Tower.

OXFORD CASTLE

On the opposite side of the road from Nuffield, once stood **Oxford Castle ❹** atop the green mound, built by Robert d'Oilly, Oxford's Norman governor, in 1071. Originally, there was a wooden keep (later rebuilt in stone) at the summit, while the outer bailey below was surrounded by a moat with water fed from the Thames – used to power the castle mills, hence Castle Mill Stream.

Many historic figures are associated with the castle. In 1142, Matilda (the Empress Maud) was holed up here for three months while battling to gain the English throne after the death of her father, Henry I, in 1135. She escaped in the depths of winter down the frozen Thames, camouflaged against the snow in nothing but a white sheet, but the unfortunate Matilda never became queen. Thereafter, the castle was used to house prisoners, and although the fortifications were torn down after the Civil War, it remained the site of a prison until 1996.

The present forbidding structure to the left of the mound was built in the 19th century. The last public execu-

The scheme also incorporates **Oxford Castle Unlocked** (tel: 01865 260 666; www.oxfordcastleunlocked. co.uk; daily 10am–5.30pm, last tour 4.20pm; charge), an attraction that includes a fascinating guided tour of **St George's Tower** and crypt as well as independent viewing of the prison D-Wing and the castle mound.

The tower was erected by Robert d'Oilly on the south side of the castle bailey in 1074, and it is worth climbing the 101 steps to the top for the views alone. Beneath the Victorian Debtors' Tower, the ancient **Crypt of the Chapel of St George**, with its fine Romanesque columns, has been opened up. It was in the original chapel that the Canons of St George established what is regarded as the first learning institution in Oxford. Finally, there is an **exhibition in D-Wing**, which presents some gruesome accounts of life and death within the prison walls.

The precinct surrounding the prison and castle has a selection of shops, restaurants and bars.

Above: slick Malmaison Hotel.

tion took place here in 1863, and the last prisoner moved out in 1993. Since then, the castle and prison complex has been redeveloped, with the main prison block converted into the smart **Malmaison Hotel** (see p.125). All guests are now of the paying variety, and most rooms consist of three cells knocked into one.

Ⓕ The Curse

During the redevelopment of the castle area, archaeologists discovered a mass grave containing the skeletons of around 60 people. A good number had been dissected before burial. Were they executed prisoners, had they succumbed to typhus, or were they even victims of the curse of Roland Jencks? At the 'Black Assizes' of 1577, this Belgian bookbinder had been convicted of supporting the Pope. In response to his punishment of being nailed by his ears to the local pillory, he laid a curse on the courtroom and city; it is said that hundreds of local men began dropping dead shortly after.

Above: the way to the prison cells – not for the squeamish.

Above: the fine colonnade inside the crypt of the Chapel of St George.

THE OLD BREWING DISTRICT

Leave the castle via the gift-shop exit on the west side, and emerging into St Thomas' Street, cross Quaking Bridge. On the opposite (south) side of the road is the former **Morrell's Brewery ❺**. Morrell's was the last brewery in Oxford, and its closure in 1998 marked the end of a long tradition. At one time, no less than 14 breweries thrived in this part of the city, drawing their water from wells deep beneath the Thames. The first brewery was established as long ago as 1452 by monks from nearby Osney Abbey *(see box opposite)*. The Brewery Gate pub next door has survived, but the brewery itself has been converted into apartments.

OXFORD CANAL

Now return to Quaking Bridge. On the corner of Lower Fisher Row is the house where Edward Tawney once lived; he ran the brewery prior to its being taken over by the Morrell family in 1792. Follow the attractive Fisher Row along Castle Mill Stream to the north, crossing Park End Street and continuing to Hythe Bridge Street and the present-day **terminus of the Oxford Canal ❻**. Here you will find a sign indicating the Oxford Canal Walk and showing the distances to towns further up the waterway.

Above: beer was brewed in Oxford ever since the first abbeys sprung up by the Thames.

River Thames. The district has nicely preserved 1850s terraces and char-acterful waterside pubs, and in the summer the river is busy with narrow boats and cruisers.

If you have a bicycle, there is a pleas-ant excursion along Binsey Lane (on the right-hand side of the Botley Road just beyond Osney), which leads out past allotments to the village of Binsey, and beyond it to St Margaret's Church with its Treacle Well *(see p.105)*.

GLOUCESTER GREEN

To continue the main route, however, head eastwards up Hythe Bridge Street towards the city. Cross the road at the traffic lights and continue on to George Street, walking past the bus station and the Old Fire Station *(see p.82)* on your

While visitors might find the 83 miles (134km) to Coventry somewhat ambi-tious, a short walk here along the tow-path, overhung by trees in the summer and lined with narrow boats, is well worthwhile. Some boats are only tem-porarily moored, whereas others have flower pots and wheelbarrows on their roofs indicating a more permanent stay. The canal continues up along the back of Worcester College *(see p.89)*, past the district of Jericho and to the edge of Port Meadow *(see p.104)*.

DETOUR TO OSNEY AND BEYOND

Back at Hythe Bridge, you have the option of a detour heading west down Hythe Bridge Street. This takes you past a number of restaurants and the **Saïd Business School** (part of the University of Oxford, opened in 2001) before the road merges with Botley Road just by the railway sta-tion. If you continue under the railway line, keeping to the south side of Bot-ley Road, a bridge (built in 1888) leads on to **Osney Island** *(see box right)*, which is surrounded by arms of the

F Osney Abbey

It is difficult to imagine today, but back in the Middle Ages, the whole of Osney Island was occupied by one of the largest Augustinian monasteries in England. Founded in 1129, but destroyed at the Dis-solution, Osney Abbey was among the first major centres of learning in Oxford. Its bell was recast as the Great Tom bell, which still chimes in Christ Church *(see p.69)*.

Above: narrow boats line up along the banks of Osney Island.

Above: the Oxford Union Society is the most famous student-run body in Britain, possibly the world, and seven of its officers have become prime ministers.

left before coming to the turning for **Gloucester Green** ❼. This large pedestrianised shopping square opened in 1989 and is now host to a market every Wednesday and an antiques and crafts market every Thursday.

Back on George Street, you are in the midst of what could be described as the entertainment heart of the city, with numerous cafés, restaurants and pubs, as well as two theatres: the New Theatre, which stages popular guest performances of theatre, ballet, musicals and opera, and the Old Fire Station, with its innovative programming in theatre, music and dance, as well as art exhibitions.

NEW INN HALL STREET

Turn right off George Street into New Inn Hall Street, heading approximately south. The original New Inn Hall, a medieval academic hall, has gone, its place taken by **St Peter's College** ❽ (tel: 01865 278 900; www.spc.ox.ac.uk; enquire at porter's lodge for access; free), which was founded in 1929 and lines the right-hand side of the street. The entrance to the college is through Linton House, the first headquarters

of the Oxford Canal Company, dating from 1797. The chapel of the college is the church of Peter-le-Bailey; rebuilt in the 18th century, it occupies the same site as the original Norman church.

OXFORD UNION

On the opposite side of the road, St Michael's Street leads back up towards Cornmarket Street. Take a short detour to peer in at the gate of the **Oxford Union** ❾ (closed to the public), which abuts the street on the right hand side. This is the great university debating club, where famous public figures are invited to argue about the issues of the day before the assembled students.

Returning to New Inn Hall Street, continue heading south. On your left, next to the entrance to Frewin Hall, is a plaque on a house, indicating that this was the **first Methodist meeting house** in Oxford. It was used as such for the first time in 1783, eight years before the death of John Wesley, who had founded the movement while at Lincoln College (see p.39).

At the end of New Inn Hall Street, you rejoin Bonn Square. Turn left to walk back up to Carfax.

E Eating Out

4500 Miles from Delhi
41 Park End Street; tel: 01865 244 922; http://milesfromdelhi.com/oxford; Mon–Fri noon–2.30pm, 5.30–11pm, Sat 5–11.30pm, Sun 5–10.30pm.
This sleek modern restaurant is not your usual Balti house, but instead aims to reinvent Indian cooking for the fine-dining crowd. The menu offers some pleasant variations from the more conventional Indian fare and dishes are subtly flavoured. There are numerous vegetarian options. ££–£££

Jamie's Italian
24–6 George Street; tel: 01865 838 383; www.jamiesitalian.com; Mon–Fri noon–11pm, Sat–Sun noon–11pm.
One in a small chain of restaurants owned by Jamie Oliver, this spacious and carefully designed establishment presents rustic Italian food with a modern twist. ££

Malmaison Brasserie
Malmaison Hotel, 3 Oxford Castle; tel: 01865 268 400; www.malmaison-oxford.com; daily breakfast, lunch and dinner.
Situated in the basement of Oxford's former prison, this stylish restaurant serves up food of a quality about as far removed as it could possibly be from the porridge once doled out to inmates. The cooking is in the modern European style and is executed with precision and care. £££

Morton's
22 New Inn Hall Street; tel: 01865 721 673; www.mortonsatwork.co.uk; 8.30am–5pm.
Superior-quality sandwich shop selling delicious baguettes and scrumptious cakes. £

Nosebag
6–8 St Michael's Street; tel: 01865 721 033; www.nosebagoxford.co.uk; daily 9.30am–9.30pm, Fri–Sat until 10pm, Sun until 8.30pm.
This is a long-standing student favourite, situated in a beautiful 15th-century building. The self-service restaurant has an unashamedly 1970s feel, with the emphasis on quiches, lasagne, salads and irresistible cakes. £–££

Zappi's Bike Café
29–32 St Michael's Street; tel: 07506 997779; http://zappisbikecafe.com; Mon–Sat 8am–5.30pm, Sun 10.30am–4pm.
Located above a bike workshop, this café serves excellent coffee and teas, cakes (including superb brownies), a range of light snacks plus various breakfast options. £

Above: dine in an old prison at Malmaison Brasserie.

Literary Oxford

Oxford has housed countless poets, novelists and playwrights, many of whom have studied there. Some have praised it, some have scorned it, and some have just drawn inspiration from it

In the university's early days, its institutions were religious halls, and most of its written output was theological or philosophical in nature. In Chaucer's *Canterbury Tales* (c.1387), *The Clerk's Tale* depicts the 'Clerke of Oxenforde' as an unworldly and impoverished bookworm, a student of philosophy and a prototype for generations of students to come.

FANTASY WRITERS

Prominent among more recent authors who have loved and celebrated Oxford are three writers of fantasy fiction: Lewis Carroll, J.R.R. Tolkien and C.S.

Lewis – all three of whom were Oxford dons. Charles Dodgson – better known as Lewis Carroll (1832–98) – was a Fellow (senior academic member) of Christ Church. He was a shy, almost reclusive man, happiest in the company of children. He grew close to Alice Liddell, the daughter of the Dean of Christ Church, and invented stories for her and her siblings, including his fantastic work, *Alice's Adventures in Wonderland*. Inspiration for the book can be glimpsed across Oxford: the Cheshire Cat sat in the bough of the tree that still graces Christ Church's Deanery Garden;

Oxford. Middle Earth can be glimpsed at the nature reserve at Risinghurst; the giant, contorted oak trees at Blenheim Park may also have given him food for creative thought.

Risinghurst made its mark, too, on C.S. Lewis (1898–1963), a fellow of Magdalen, for this is where he invented his magical world of Narnia (*The Chronicles of Narnia*, published 1950–56). Both Tolkien and Lewis met up with fellow members of the Inklings Group in the venerable Eagle and Child pub.

THE CITY IN FICTION

Oxford itself has enjoyed a starring role in numerous works, including Thomas Hardy's *Jude the Obscure*, in which the ill-fated protagonist aspires to break through the class barriers and study in the city of dreaming spires. It is the setting for *Zuleika Dobson* (1911), a satire of undergraduate life by Merton alumnus Max Beerbohm (1872–1956), and for Evelyn Waugh's (1903–66) *Brideshead Revisited* (1945), with its romanticised view of privileged college life. There are many references to the city in Whitbread Prize-winner Philip Pullman's (b.1946) *His Dark Materials* trilogy, and Oxford is well represented in the crime genre by Colin Dexter (b.1930), creator of Inspector Morse (novels published 1975–99), Veronica Stallwood and Dorothy L. Sayers.

the Treacle Well is still at Binsey and both 'the loveliest garden you ever saw' and a tunnel that gave Carroll the idea for the one down which Alice falls are at Worcester College.

J.R.R. Tolkien (1892–1973), who studied at Exeter College and was Professor at Pembroke and Merton, also found inspiration for *The Hobbit* (1937) and *The Lord of the Rings* (1954–5) in

WRITERS AT ODDS WITH OXFORD

Not that it has been smooth sailing for all Oxford-educated writers. In 1729 Samuel Johnson was sent down (expelled) from Pembroke because he couldn't pay his bills. Percy Bysshe Shelley's time at University College ended in 1811 when he was expelled for publishing a pamphlet in defence of atheism. And John Betjeman – a student of C.S. Lewis – was thrown out of Magdalen for failing a divinity exam in 1927.

Above: *The Golden Compass*, based on Philip Pullman's *His Dark Materials* trilogy. **Top left**: *Brideshead Revisited* is set in Oxford. **Bottom left**: The Mad Hatter and the March Hare at their tea party. **Left**: Colin Dexter invented Inspector Morse.

Jericho and St Giles'

Spend the morning in the Ashmolean Museum, have a relaxing lunch in Jericho, then wander along St Giles' before finishing up in the pub

This route of a little over a mile begins by exploring past civilisations in the Ashmolean Museum before entering the district of Jericho to discover the city's publishing heritage. And publishing remains the theme as the walk wends its way back to St Giles', where the Eagle and Child pub was a meeting place of some famous authors.

Highlights

- Ashmolean Museum
- Worcester College
- Jericho
- Little Clarendon Street shops and cafés
- The Eagle and Child pub

ASHMOLEAN MUSEUM

Looking across from the Martyrs' Memorial, the entrance to Beaumont Street is dominated on the left by the famous **Randolph Hotel** (see p.95), a splendid Victorian-Gothic edifice dating from 1863, and on the right by the neo-Grecian facade of the **Taylor Institute**. The four statues standing on the tops of the columns represent France, Germany, Italy and Spain, for the institute was founded for the study of the languages of these four countries. The Taylor Institute forms the east wing of the **Ashmolean Museum** ❶ (tel: 01865 278 000; www.ashmol.ox.ac. uk; Tue–Sun 10am–6pm; free), the main facade of which stretches along the north side of Beaumont Street.

Left and Above: the prestigious Ashmolean Museum.

History

Built in 1841–5 and containing the University of Oxford's collections of art and antiquities, the Ashmolean is the oldest museum in the country. Set up by the antiquary and scholar Elias Ashmole in 1683, its first home was in purpose-built premises on Broad Street (now the Museum of the History of Science, see p.15). But the origin of the collection goes back to before Ashmole's day, and not to Oxford, but to Lambeth, London. There, in a pub called The Ark, the early 17th-century naturalist and royal gardener John Tradescant displayed his extensive collection of rarities and curiosities, either gathered by himself on his trips to Europe or given to him by sea captains. After his death in 1638, Tradescant's son, also called John, expanded the collection with items from the New World, specifically Virginia, to which he travelled on several occasions.

Meanwhile, Ashmole had befriended the Tradescants and persuaded them that he would be a suitable curator for their curiosities after their deaths. The younger Tradescant left a contradictory will bequeathing the collection to both Oxford and Cambridge, which his widow and Ashmole challenged. Ashmole won, in time, and in return for an

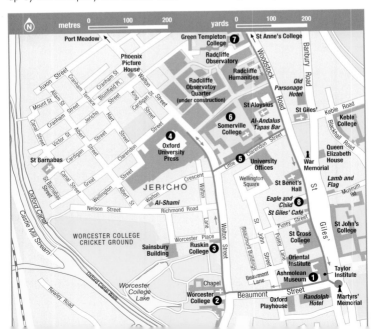

Above: the Ashmolean's granite macehead of king Scorpion, dating back to the 1st dynasty c.3100 BC.

hawking gear, a rhinoceros-horn cup from China, and, as the star attraction, Powhattan's Mantle. Powhattan was the king of Virginia, and the father of Pocahontas (of Disney film fame).

Antiquities

Since moving to Beaumont Street, the Ashmolean has developed into one of the world's great museums, hugely enriched by archaeological material, given by such notable excavators as Sir Flinders Petrie, the Egyptologist, and Sir Arthur Evans, who discovered the palace of Knossos on Crete.

In 2009, the museum reopened after a £60-million redevelopment. Behind the original 1845 Cockerell Building, a new gallery space was created, doubling the capacity with 39 more galleries plus an education centre and rooftop restaurant. The design, by architect Rick Mather, also features interlinking glass-enclosed walkways and airy stairwells ranging over five floors.

honorary degree, he passed it (and his coin collection) to Oxford.

Items from the original 'Ark' are on display in room 8 on the lower ground floor. It is a wonderfully eclectic group of objects, including Guy Fawkes's lantern, Oliver Cromwell's death mask, a piece of the stake at which Bishop Latimer was burned *(see p.22 and 35)*, as well as Henry VIII's stirrups and

The museum has completely reorganised its exhibits, bringing the interaction of civilisations and cultures to the fore. Thus, on the Ancient World (ground) floor, objects dating from pre-history to 700 AD plot the emer-

Ⓕ Alfred's Jewel

In case P307 in gallery 41 on the second floor (England 400–1600) is the museum's most famous exhibit, the Alfred Jewel. Found in Somerset in 1693, it is regarded as the finest piece of Saxon art ever discovered. Consisting of an enamel seated figure, set under a rock crystal in a gold frame, bearing the inscription *Aelfred mec heht gewyrcan* ('Alfred had me made'), it is in fact not an item of personal jewellery, but instead would have been affixed to a pointer used for following the text of a manuscript.

Above: the exquisite Alfred Jewel, late 9th century AD.

Above: Lucien Pissarro's *Eragny Church* hangs in the Ashmolean.

gence and flowering of ancient cultures from Egypt and the Near East, through Greece and Rome, to India and China, a theme continued on the next floor with coverage of the Silk Road. Art occupies the upper levels. Don't miss the drawings by Michelangelo and Raphael, as well as *The Hunt in the Forest*, painted by the Florentine Paolo Uccello in 1466. There are also more recent works by pre-Raphaelite and Impressionist artists.

FORMER ROYAL PALACE

Leaving the Ashmolean, turn right (west) along Beaumont Street. Now lined by terraces of fine Regency houses, the western end of this street was at one time occupied by Beaumont Palace, built in the early 12th century by Henry I as his royal residence in Oxford, and the birthplace of his sons Richard (the Lionheart) and John. Though the palace represented the town's rise in importance during the early Middle Ages, it did not remain here for long; the original door was already available for architectural salvage when the founders of Merton acquired it for

their library entrance, where it can still be seen today *(see p.48)*.

WORCESTER COLLEGE

At the end of Beaumont Street, cross the road to visit **Worcester College** ❷ (tel: 01865 278 300; www.worc. ox.ac.uk; daily 2–5pm; free). Worcester is different from most other colleges in that it has no intimate, enclosed

Above: the crest of one of Worcester College's founding abbeys.

Above: walking through the serene cloister at Worcester College.

quadrangles. But this in no way detracts from the appeal of the place, for as well as some fine architecture, the college boasts beautiful gardens.

The college fabric

Although founded in the early 18th century, the origins of the college go back to Gloucester Hall, which was established here for Benedictine monks in 1283, but dissolved in about 1539. After the Dissolution, Gloucester continued as an academic hall, despite several Benedictine changes of ownership, but slid into debt and decline. The doorheads of the west range bear the coat of arms, carved in stone, of the principal abbeys connected with the college: Glastonbury, Malmesbury, Canterbury and Pershore.

Revival only came at the end of the 17th century with funds provided by Sir Thomas Cookes, a Worcestershire baronet. The new Worcester College received its statutes in 1714, but the 18th-century building programme was financed by another man, George Clarke, who is remembered by the college as *tantum nos Fundator* ('almost our Founder').

Despite this injection of money, Worcester was never very wealthy, and the original Gloucester Hall's medieval cottages owe their survival to the fact that the college could only afford the two neoclassical ranges we see today. Of these, the front or west range is the most interesting, for it contains the Library (above the cloister), the Hall and the chapel (in the two wings).

Above: the highly regarded 1982 Sainsbury Building, on the Worcester College grounds.

Designed by Nicholas Hawksmoor, the library was founded on a substantial collection of books and manuscripts donated by George Clarke, and includes a large proportion of the surviving drawings of Inigo Jones. The Hall and chapel were completed by James Wyatt in the 1770s. Both were transformed internally by William Burges in the latter half of the 19th century. The hall was, controversially, restored to its 18th-century appearance in 1966, but the chapel remains as a splendid example of Burges' highly unusual style. Sadly, the gloom created by the dark stained glass prevents a full appreciation of the lavish interior, with its Roman-style floor mosaics, Raphaelesque frescoes and gilded ceiling. Evangelists fill the niches at each corner of the chapel, and the pew ends are carved with a menagerie of animals and birds.

The gardens

Worcester is sited on a slope, the land dropping away to the west. A tunnel at the end of the Gloucester Hall cottages leads through to the gardens, which are as beautiful as any in Oxford, a fact endorsed by Lewis Carroll in *Alice's Adventures in Wonderland*, where he describes the tunnel 'not much larger than a rathole' leading 'to the loveliest garden you ever saw'.

Landscaped like a small park, the gardens are planted with magnificent trees and shrubs and include a picturesque willow-fringed lake. They were laid out in the early 19th century after the completion of the Oxford Canal (1790), which now forms the western boundary of the college grounds. A walk around the lake is highly recommended.

Looking back through the trees there are glimpses of the magnificent Palladian facade of the Provost's House, while at the northern end of the lake is the **Sainsbury Building**, built in 1982. Regarded as one of the best pieces of modern architecture in Oxford, its carefully juxtaposed roof lines and walls descend to a delightful lakeside terrace. The college playing fields stretch away to the north.

Above: the lovely landscaped gardens at Worcester College inspired Lewis Carroll.

Above: the Oxford University Press Museum displays many printing artefacts relating to its history.

TOWN MEETS GOWN

Leaving Worcester by the main gate, now walk north along Walton Street. On the corner of Worcester Place stands **Ruskin College ❸**. Not strictly part of the university, this is one of a number of institutions founded in memory of the art (and later social) critic, John Ruskin, for the education of working men and women. The college has strong links with the trade union movement and the Workers' Educational Association. Among its most illustrious alumni is the former Deputy Prime Minister, John Prescott.

Ruskin is appropriately sited on the edge of the former working-class suburb of Jericho. Some say that the name derives from the insubstantial nature of the jerry-built terraced houses, a few of which date to the 1830s. There was, however, a pub called the Jericho House here as early as 1688, and the name was used in the 17th century for any remote place, by analogy with the biblical town in Palestine.

The area was developed in the early 18th century to house the increasing numbers of workers in this part of the city, after the arrival of the Oxford Canal in 1790. When **Oxford University**

Press ❹ (situated in a grand neoclassical building just round the first corner) moved here from the Clarendon Building in 1830, further houses were built to accommodate the print workers. And it was the print workers who made up the majority of the congregation of the **Church of St Barnabas**, which was built by the canal in 1868. You can get to the church and take in some of the atmosphere of old Jericho by taking a stroll down Great Clarendon Street. The church is distinctive for its tall, Italian-Romanesque style tower which dominates the district.

To learn more about the history of this world-famous publishing house, make an appointment to see the OUP Museum (*see box below*).

❺ The Oxford Book

The Oxford University Press Museum (tel: 01865 267 527; Mon–Fri 10am–4pm) is a small museum which preserves and displays the historic books, documents and printing equipment of the Oxford University Press. Graphic panels tell the story of 'The Oxford Book' from the 15th century to the CD-Rom. The Museum's most priceless possession is the first edition of Lord Clarendon's *History of the Great Rebellion*.

Above: the museum's most prized possession, the first edition of the *History of the Great Rebellion*.

Above: Ruskin College is not part of the University of Oxford, but has been granted special privileges.

FROM RAGS TO RICHES

Featured as the cholera-ridden slum of Beersheba in Thomas Hardy's *Jude the Obscure*, Jericho's working-class credentials have long expired, for its prime location at the threshold to the city has made it a desirable area to live, particularly for wealthy students and young professionals. House prices have soared and Walton Street is now lined with craft shops, boutiques, delicatessens and restaurants. Opposite the Press building is the neo-Grecian facade of **the old St Paul's Church**, built in 1835. It no longer functions as a church but as Freud, a wine bar and restaurant with live-music programmes specialising in jazz *(see p.95)*.

If you continue along Walton Street, past the **Phoenix Picture House** and the Brasserie Blanc, you soon reach Walton Well Road on your left, which leads over the canal and railway line to the vast expanse of Port Meadow *(see p.104)*. Otherwise, head back to **Little Clarendon Street ❺**, which links Walton Street with St Giles'. Amongst buildings housing the university's administrative offices, there are numerous bars, brasseries and cafés situated cheek by jowl with a number of boutiques, galleries, furniture stores and gift shops.

SOMERVILLE COLLEGE

Emerging on to St Giles', now turn left and head northwards as the road becomes Woodstock Road. Before long, on your left is the **Oratory Church of St Aloysius**, where Mass is still celebrated every Sunday in Latin. Just beyond the Oratory is the entrance to **Somerville College ❻** (tel: 01865 270 600; www.some.ox.ac.uk; daily 2–4.30pm; free) which though founded in 1859, was not – in common with the other four women's halls founded in the late 19th century – recognised as a full college until 1959. Despite this handicap, Somerville has educated an extraordinary number of female public figures, including Margaret Thatcher and Indira Gandhi. It now also admits male undergraduates and graduates.

Above: the tower of St Barnabas, with its Italian campanile looks, stands out from other church towers in Oxford.

K St Giles' Fair

For two days every September (the Monday and Tuesday following the first Sunday of the month) St Giles' is the scene of the St Giles' Fair. Cherished by people of all ages and backgrounds, this colourful fair has origins dating back to a parish wake first recorded in 1624.

Above: the traditional carousel takes pride of place at St Giles' Fair.

ELUSIVE OBSERVATORY

Further along Woodstock Road, not far beyond the Radcliffe Infirmary, you will reach **Green Templeton College** ❼ (tel: 01865 274 770; www.gtc. ox.ac.uk; enquire at the porter's lodge for access), founded only in 2008 after the merger of the medically orientated Green College and the management science orientated Templeton. This youngest of colleges has absorbed into its precinct the famous **Radcliffe Observatory**, designed by James Wyatt and completed in 1794, and described by Nikolaus Pevsner as 'architecturally the finest observatory in Europe'. Unfortunately, it can no longer generally be visited by the public. However, you can get close enough to see that the top half of the building, with its octagonal shape and zodiacal signs (this version also topped by Hercules and Atlas holding up the Globe) is reminiscent of the Tower of the Winds in Athens.

The observatory has lent its name to the **Radcliffe Observatory Project**, a major University development just to the south, due for completion in 2013.

ST GILES'

Now return back down Woodstock Road into St Giles'. This broad boulevard runs between the War Memorial and St Giles' Church in the north to the Martyrs' Memorial in the south. The church is largely 13-century and sits in an island of green, facing down the wide, tree-lined thoroughfare, best seen in early September when the traffic is excluded for the annual St Giles' Fair *(see box left)*.

The right-hand side (west) of St Giles' is lined with many attractive 17th- and 18th-century houses, some accommodating religious institutions, including the Christian Scientists at Nos 34–6, St Benet's Hall for Benedictine monks at No. 38 and the Quakers at No. 43. Just beyond Pusey Street, St Cross College is an Anglican theological college.

Perhaps the most interesting building on the western side of St Giles', however, is the **Eagle and Child pub**

Above: the Eagle and Child was also a regular watering-hole for Colin Dexter, creator of Inspector Morse.

8 *(see below)*, on the corner of Wellington Place. It has been an inn since at least 1650, but its fame rests on the literary group known as the Inklings, which met up here in the so-called Rabbit Room (which now displays related memorabilia) between 1939 and 1962. Headed by C.S. Lewis, the group also included such luminaries as J.R.R. Tolkien and Charles Williams.

It was here, in these cosy, fireside surroundings that Tolkien began discussing his fantasy saga *The Lord of the Rings*, little realising that it would become such a world-wide success that he would be forced, by a torrent of letters, phone calls and visits from excited fans, to exchange the comforts of Oxford for a life of seclusion in Bournemouth.

Above: renowned chef Raymond Blanc owns several eateries in and outside Oxford.

E Eating Out

Al Andalus Tapas Bar
10 Little Clarendon Street; tel: 01865 516 688; www.tapasoxford.co.uk; Mon–Thur noon–3pm, 5pm–late, Fri–Sun noon–late.
Lively Spanish restaurant offering tapas, paellas, larger meat dishes, and salads. The special lunch menu is particularly good value for money. ££

Al Shami
25 Walton Crescent; tel: 01865 310 066; www.al-shami.co.uk; daily noon–midnight.
This excellent Lebanese restaurant offers a large menu that includes mezze, fish dishes and charcoal grills. Plenty of vegetarian options. £–££

Eagle and Child
49 St Giles'; tel: 01865 302 925; daily noon–11pm.
This quintessentially Oxfordian hostelry (now owned by St John's College) serves up traditional pub grub: hearty pies, fish and chips, Ploughman's salad, sausage and mash, and good Sunday roasts. Make room too for the school dinner-style desserts such as chocolate pudding and apple crumble. £–££

Freud
Walton Street; tel: 01865 311 171; www.freud.eu; daily 11am until late.
Something of an institution, this fashionable café-bar is housed in a cavernous neoclassical church. The food (mainly homemade pizzas) isn't exceptional, but in the evenings there are cocktails, and often live jazz. £–££

Randolph Hotel Restaurant
Randolph Hotel, Beaumont Street; tel: 0844 879 9132; www.macdonald hotels.co.uk/randolph.
This is grand old-fashioned dining: a baronial-style hall, starched white table cloths and impeccably smart waiting staff. The food is good too, combining the very best Scottish butchery or fresh fish with local organic vegetables and dairy produce. £££

St Giles' Café
52 St Giles'; tel: 07918 775421; Mon–Sat 8am–3pm, Sun 9am–3pm.
This classic greasy spoon café has not changed in decades, serving an excellent full English with a mug of coffee. £

Tour 9

St John's and the North

In the space of a day, this 1½-mile (2.4km) walk takes in fossilised dinosaurs, Oxford's richest college, pubs, punting, and perhaps even first-class cricket in the University Parks

Starting in St Giles', this route explores the area immediately to the north of the city centre, which was developed after the great university reforms in the mid-19th century. The route also includes two wonderful museums and a glorious park, and passes by several historic pubs along the way.

ST JOHN'S COLLEGE

From the Martyrs' Memorial, follow the east side of St Giles' to the entrance of **St John's College ❶** (tel: 01865 277 300; www.sjc.ox.ac.uk; daily 1–5pm; free). Founded in 1457 for Cistercian monks and originally named after St Bernard, the college was refounded after the Dissolution by Sir Thomas White, who was a

Highlights

- St John's College
- Keble College
- Punting on the Cherwell River
- Dinosaurs at the University Museum
- Shrunken heads in the Pitt Rivers Museum
- University Parks

member of the wealthy Merchant Taylor's guild. He renamed the college St John's after the patron saint of tailors. It remains one of the wealthiest colleges in Oxford, with an endowment worth several hundred million pounds. Indeed it is sometimes said that you can walk all the way from Oxford to

Left: punts lined up ready for hire.
Above: St John's College is one of the richest in Oxford.

Cambridge on land owned by St John's. It is also notable as the college where Tony Blair spent his student days.

The niche on the gate-tower is occupied by St Bernard, while that on the inner side of the tower contains a superb modern statue of St John the Baptist, created by Eric Gill in 1936. Apart from this addition, most of the **front quad** dates to the time of the college's foundation.

Passing through the archway to the east, however, the visitor jumps two centuries into the magnificent **Canterbury Quad**. Built by the little-known architect Adam Browne, this magnificent Baroque quadrangle was financed by Archbishop Laud, famous as the university chancellor responsible for drawing up stringent rules governing the behaviour and dress of scholars that remained in force until more progressive ideologies took over in the 1850s.

Straight ahead, flanked by a fine Tuscan-style arcade, a two-storey portal contains a bronze statue of Charles I. He faces a similar statue of his wife, Queen Henrietta Maria, housed in a niche on the opposite side. When the

quad was completed in 1636, both were invited to attend the opening ceremony, which is said to have cost more than the buildings themselves.

Beyond the quad, the archway leads through to **the gardens**. Like neighbouring Trinity College (see p.36), St John's was built outside the city walls and so the gardens are very spacious. The path around the lawn twists and turns between carefully tended shrubs and groves of trees, providing a wonderful blend of the formal and the naturalistic. Visitors can extend their walk by taking a side path to the

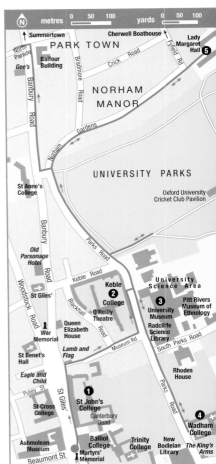

F The O'Reilly Theatre

The entrance to the O'Reilly Theatre, opened in 2002, can be found on Blackhall Road, at the back of Keble College. The 180-seat auditorium hosts student productions during term times and a programme of talks by famous actors and other luminaries of the theatre. Tickets can usually be bought on the door, though check the website for full details (www.oreillytheatre.co.uk).

Above: check out Keble College's O'Reilly Theatre.

north, past rockeries and shady lawns, catching glimpses of more modern college buildings (including the so-called 'Fish-tank on stilts') at the extremities of the college grounds.

KEBLE COLLEGE

As you leave St John's turn right up St Giles'. At the **Lamb and Flag pub** (see Eating Out, p.103), a passageway takes the visitor from the Middle Ages to the 19th century, emerging as it does, via Museum Road, on to Parks Road, which was first laid out in the 1830s. Directly opposite stands the impressive neo-Gothic facade of the University Museum. But before crossing the road, turn left up Parks Road to arrive at the entrance to the enormous brick edifice that is **Keble College** ❷ (tel: 01865 272 727; www.keble. ox.ac.uk; summer 10am–7pm, winter

10–5pm; free). Founded in 1868 as a memorial to John Keble, who inspired the Oxford Movement (see p.23), the college was created as a bastion of High Church traditionalism at a time when the rest of the university was undergoing massive liberalising reforms. Initially students had to lead an almost monastic life of poverty and obedience. The Tractarian founders of the college chose one of their own, William Butterfield, as the architect, who proceeded to produce a riot of Victorian Gothic on a scale hitherto unseen.

Controversial from the very beginning, Keble continues to attract its fair share of criticism. It was built not of Oxford stone, but of brick, and in addition to the dominant red, Butterfield used other colours to create his hallmark polychromatic patterning. Nowhere are the aspirations of the college's creators more evident than in the enormous chapel, visited not generally for its slightly kitsch mosaics and stained glass, but for Holman Hunt's famous painting The Light of the World, which hangs in a side chapel to the south. Butterfield refused to

Above: William Butterfield's contentious red-bricked facade for Keble College.

Above: University Museum's dinosaur collection.

allow the picture to be hung in the main chapel on the grounds that it is 'a place of worship, not a gallery'. Holman Hunt, on the other hand, was so angry when he learned that the college was charging visitors to see the picture that he painted another and gave it to St Paul's Cathedral in London.

The mixed voice choir of Keble College not only sings in the Chapel at services on Wednesday and Sunday evenings but also tours throughout Britain, Europe and the US, and has recorded several CDs.

UNIVERSITY MUSEUM

Opposite Keble College stands another neo-Gothic temple of sorts, the **University Museum** ❸ (tel: 01865 272 950; www.oum.ox.ac.uk; daily 10am–5pm; free). Supported by some of the most famous progressive thinkers of the day (including John Ruskin), work began on this natural history museum in 1855. The design was highly controversial because the Gothic style was thought to be inappropriate for a secular structure, but there can be no denying the splendour of the interior.

Ⓖ University Parks: Horticulture and Cricket

North of Keble, long summer days attract locals and visitors alike to the huge expanse of the University Parks. Dotted with superb trees and shrubs and bordered on its eastern side by the River Cherwell, the park is a wonderful place for a stroll. It is also the home of the Oxford University Cricket Club, and one of only two places in England (the other is Cambridge) where first-class matches can be watched free of charge.

Above: game in play at the Oxford University Cricket Club.

Above: the main entrance to the University Museum.

The central aisle of the main hall is dominated by the fine skeleton of an iguanodon, whose rib structure appears to be repeated in the wrought-iron vaulting of the glass roof. Slender iron columns divide the hall into three bays; the arcade columns around the sides are each hewn from a different British rock. Surrounding the hall are the statues of eminent scientists,

while further embellishment is provided by stone carvings of plants, birds and animals (created by the brothers O'Shea from Dublin).

Apart from the dinosaurs, a famous attraction of the museum is the painting by John Savery of the Dodo in the northwest corner of the building. The bird in question, described as an oversized flightless dove with a hooked beak, was brought to England in 1638 and formed part of the Tradescant and subsequently Ashmolean collections *(see p.86)*. The same painting inspired Lewis Carroll's famous character in *Alice in Wonderland*. It is also well worth visiting the upper gallery for its fine collections of insects, butterflies and birds; notice the scale model of the sun, moon and earth attached to the balustrade.

PITT RIVERS MUSEUM

If you are impressed by the University Museum, then you will be even more surprised by what lies beyond, through the doors to the rear. **The Pitt Rivers Museum of Ethnology** (tel: 01865 270 927; www.prm.ox.ac.uk; Mon noon–4.30pm, Tue–Sun 10am–4.30pm; free) was built in 1885 to house the col-

Ⓕ Descended from Monkeys?

When the University Museum was completed in 1860, the great 19th-century debate on the validity of Darwin's evolutionary theories was in full swing. At the inaugural ceremony, there was a confrontation on the issue between Samuel Wilberforce, the Bishop of Oxford, and Thomas Huxley, the eminent biologist and Darwin's most strident supporter. At one point, the bishop turned to Huxley and asked 'was it through his grandfather or grandmother that he claimed descent from a monkey?'

Above: Charles Darwin.

Above: the main vaulted hall of the University Museum is impressive by its sheer height alone.

lection of Lieutenant-General Augustus Henry Lane Pitt Rivers, built up during his service in exotic lands with the Grenadier Guards. The original collection consisted of some 15,000 objects, but since then the number has swelled to well over a million, of which some 400,000 are on permanent display. The exotic exhibits come from all corners of the earth – scary demons, potent fertility figures, colourful totem poles and exotic masks – as well as practical objects such as boats, tents, saddles and snowshoes.

A remarkable theme of the museum is the continuity and similarities that exist between cultures; illuminating parallels are drawn between the use of magical charms among the tribes of Asia and similar practices among Christians in 'civilised' Europe. To help achieve this, and in accordance with Pitt Rivers' wishes, the objects are displayed not by region but by type, so model Chinese junks are to be found next to African dug-out canoes, etc. There is a cabinet containing the shrunken heads of Ecua-

dorian Indians, complete with instructions on head shrinking. Attendants will point out all kinds of other ghoulish delights, including drawers full of giant toads, and a witch in a bottle.

When you step outside again, examine the lawn in front of the University Museum: casts of megalosaurus footprints have been set into the turf – exact replicas of those unearthed at Audley Quarry to the north of Oxford.

WADHAM COLLEGE

From the University Museum, head south down Parks Road towards Broad Street. On the left is **Wadham College ❹** (tel: 01865 277 900; www.wadham.ox.ac.uk; 1–4.15pm term time; out of term time 10.30–11.45am, 1–4.15pm; free). Built in 1609–13, it is the youngest of Oxford's pre-Victorian foundations. Nicholas Wadham, a retiring and obscure Somerset landowner, left his considerable wealth for the foundation of a college at his death in 1609. Wadham's widow, Dorothy, proved an energetic executor, despite being over 75 years old, and by 1613,

Above: exotic mask from the Pitt Rivers Museum collection.

ⓖ Messing About in Boats

Following Bardwell and Chadrington roads just to the north of Park Town, prospective punters can head for the Cherwell Boathouse, with its elegant restaurant of the same name *(see Eating Out, opposite)*. There are plenty of punts for hire, and you might consider heading north along the Cherwell as far as Marston Ferry, where there is no longer a ferry across the river but where the Victoria Arms is an ideal spot for a pub lunch or a long summer evening after a picnic on the river.

Above: punting is a delightful way to explore Oxford.

Below: the Jacobean-Gothic front quad at Wadham College.

less than five years later, the college was virtually complete. Thus Wadham is the only ancient college to have been built at one go, and it has scarcely changed.

The front quad is distinguished by its fine Jacobean-Gothic portal, a scaled-down version of the Tower of the Five Orders in the Old Schools Quadrangle *(see p.18)*. The chapel contains some fine stained glass including the magnificent east window by Bernard von Linge (1822), brother of the more famous Abraham.

Beyond lies the wonderfully serene **Fellows' Garden**, filled with rare and ancient trees, the perfect environment in the 1650s for mathematicians and scientists such as Christopher Wren and Robert Boyle to meet up and discuss their theories; they later moved on to London to found the Royal Society.

TOWARDS NORTH OXFORD

As you leave Wadham, you have the option of an early finish to the tour – by returning straight to the city centre to the south – or you can explore some of the area to the north of the University Parks and Museum by walking up Parks Road and beyond. This affluent district, now known as North Oxford, extends out along the Banbury and Woodstock roads and came into being partly as a result of the university's expansion during the latter half of the 19th century.

Just north of the Parks, the elaborate neo-Gothic villas of **Norham Gardens** were built to house professors and their families, who now had the freedom to reside outside college. At the end of Norham Gardens (also reached via an alley from University Parks) is **Lady Margaret Hall ❺** (tel: 01865 274 300; www.lmh.ox.ac. uk; enquire at the porter's lodge for access), founded in 1878 as a women's hall of residence (it is now mixed) and itself occupying one of the newly built villas. There have been a number of notable extensions since, including the Byzantine-style chapel designed by Sir Giles Gilbert Scott in 1931.

For a change of style, return to the Banbury Road and walk north for about 400m/yds to Park Town, a much-admired residential crescent built in the 1850s, the Regency style of which seems more akin to Cheltenham than Oxford.

NORTH PARADE

Just to the south of Park Town, on the opposite side of the Banbury Road, is North Parade, a narrow lane which has more the atmosphere of a village than a city. It has a variety of restaurants as well as two good pubs, the Gardeners' Arms and the Rose and Crown, the latter built in 1867 on the site of a small market garden, evidence of the area's semi-rural charac-

Above: Wadham College's chapel, noted for its 17th-century stained glass.

ter at the time. However, there is no satisfactory explanation as to why this lane should be called North Parade – when South Parade is situated a mile to the north in Summertown.

ⓔ Eating Out

Cherwell Boathouse
Bardwell Road; tel: 01865 552 746; www.cherwellboathouse.co.uk; daily noon–2.30pm and 6.30–9.30pm.
Set in an idyllic location on the river, the Cherwell Boathouse comprises a restaurant, bar and punt-hire company. The restaurant's food is modern European in style and is based on seasonal local produce. £££

Gee's Restaurant
61 Banbury Road; tel: 01865 553 540; www.gees-restaurant.co.uk; lunch: daily noon–2.30pm, Sun till 3.30pm; dinner: daily 6pm–10pm, Fri–Sat till 10.30pm.
One of Oxford's best and most atmospheric restaurants in a former flower glass house. The food is modern British and relies on top quality seasonal produce, much of it from the owner's Oxfordshire farm. £££

Lamb and Flag
12 St Giles'; tel: 01865 515 787; daily noon–11pm, food lunchtimes only.

Like the Eagle and Child opposite, this pub is owned by St John's College. The beer is good and the food is standard pub fare. £

Luna Caprese
4 North Parade; tel: 01865 554 812; daily noon–2pm, 6–11pm.
This long-established Italian restaurant is impervious to fads, and justifiably so, given the consistent quality of the food. The walls are decked with fishing nets and shells, the pasta is always freshly made, if it is your birthday, the Italian waiters may even sing for you. ££

Saffron
204–206 Banbury Road; tel: 01865 512 211; www.saffronatoxford.co.uk; Mon–Sat noon–2.30pm and 5.30–11.30pm; all day Sun.
Top-quality Indian fare, the innovative menu including a good range of unusual dishes with distinctive flavours. Excellent service; buffet lunch on Sundays. £–££

Tour 10

Port Meadow and Beyond

Escape the hubbub of the city with a walk through the glorious Port Meadow alongside the Thames, to the Trout pub, 4 miles (6.5km) away

If you walk northwards along Walton Street *(see p.92)*, and then turn left down Walton Well Road, you come to a **bridge** that crosses the railway and canal and leads to one of Oxford's most beautiful and enduring treasures, the 400-acre (160-hectare) expanse of **Port Meadow ❶**.

Used continuously for grazing ever since its first mention in the Domesday Book (1087), the meadow is a rare piece of Old England; it has never once been ploughed over, and today visitors are still usually outnumbered by horses and cattle. This pristine meadow is also rich in birdlife and wild flowers. Annual winter floods bring spectacular flocks of wildfowl and waders, and the meadow is a magnet for migrating birds, with Canada geese taking off and landing in

Highlights

• The flora and fauna of Port Meadow
• The Perch pub
• The Treacle Well, near Binsey
• The remains of Godstow Nunnery
• The Trout pub

their hundreds. In summer, you can often make out the outlines of Iron Age farming enclosures and hut circles, delineated by the buttercups that grow taller over buried features such as ditches and foundation trenches.

ACROSS THE MEADOW

Visitors can wander all over the meadow as long as they do not pick the wild flowers. But a popular route

Left and Above: kayaking and walking in Port Meadow make for a wonderful break away from the city centre bustle.

follows the main path across to the Thames. At the first bridge, an arm of the river is used for mooring house-boats and leisure craft, and the bank is popular with children who want to feed the ducks, swans and geese on the other side. The Thames itself is crossed a little further upstream over a **steel-arched bridge**, and if you continue past the sailing club, a path on the left leads to the village of **Binsey**, with its popular pub, **The Perch ❷** (see p.107).

TREACLE WELL

To the north of Binsey, a narrow lane leads for about half a mile to **St Margaret's Church**, where the principal attraction is the **Treacle Well ❸**, described by the Door-mouse at the Mad Hatter's Tea Party in Lewis Carroll's *Alice's Adventures in Wonderland*. The well is also associated with the story of St Frideswide, Oxford's patron saint. Her suitor, the King of Wessex, was struck blind when he tried to carry her away, but

ⒼFrom Perch to Trout

A fun way to follow a good portion of this route – from The Perch to The Trout – is to hire a boat. Oxford River Cruises (tel: 0845 226 9396; www.oxfordrivercruises.com) operate from moorings at the bottom of the garden of The Perch pub. Visitors can hire rowing boats, punts, canoes, and even (if you are feeling lazy) electric launches. When you reach The Trout, you can make fast your vessel and disembark for a refreshing pint before sailing back again.

Above: The Perch attracts large crowds of Sunday walkers.

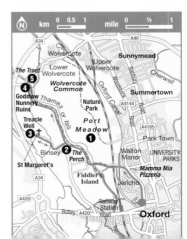

Above: the remains of medieval Godstow Nunnery.

she agreed to cure him on condition that he leave her in peace. The well miraculously appeared and its waters restored the king's sight. The name 'treacle' commemorates this miracle; in Middle English, 'triacle' signified any liquid with healing or medicinal properties – only later did it come to mean syrup.

Hundreds of pilgrims used to visit St Margaret's. Few come now and the rustic nave, lit only by oil lamps has

Above: peeking into the Treacle Well at the Church of St Margaret, Binsey.

been colonised by bats. The simple wooden pulpit has a carving of St Margaret trampling on a dragon. There is another relief of St Margaret on the pulpit's inside – not by Eric Gill, as has been claimed – with clearly delineated breasts. Regarded as rather too sensual, she is condemned to face the feet of the incumbent preacher rather than risk arousing the passions of the congregation.

GODSTOW NUNNERY

Returning to the path along the Thames, continue the walk north, and after about a mile you reach Godstow Lock and the **remains of Godstow Nunnery** ❹. Founded in 1138 by Benedictine monks, the nunnery is now a romantic ruin. It was here that Rosamund Clifford, mistress of King Henry II, was buried in 1175. According to legend, 'fair Rosamund' was murdered by the jealous Queen Eleanor, but the truth is probably less melodramatic – she seems to have retired to the nunnery when Henry finally grew bored with her.

Godstow was also the destination of Charles Dodgson (alias Lewis Carroll) as, together with a friend, he rowed Alice Liddell and her two sisters for a picnic at the lock, in the summer of 1862. It was while they were rowing that Dodgson recited to them for the first time the lines that subsequently appeared at the beginning of *Alice's Adventures in Wonderland*:

All in the golden afternoon
Full leisurely we glide;
For both our oars,
with little skill,
By little arms are plied,
While little hands make vain pretence
Our wanderings to guide.

Nearby, **The Trout** ❺, originally a fisherman's cottage, was rebuilt in 1737. The pub overlooks a roaring weir and a wooden footbridge over the river, and peacocks and swans are often to be seen in the grounds. It is a popular place on long summer evenings, but nice also in winter with its roaring log fires. The easiest way back to Oxford is the way you came, but the weary can follow the road over the river to Wolvercote, and then either follow the canal towpath or take a bus or taxi back to the city centre.

🄴 Eating Out

Mamma Mia Pizzeria
102 Walton Street; tel: 01865 311 211; www.mammamiapizzeria.co.uk; Mon–Fri noon–3pm and 5–10.30pm, Sat–Sun noon–10.30pm.
Well-run and reliable restaurant serving some of the best pizzas in Oxford as well as excellent starters, salads and pasta dishes. Sister restaurant to the long-established Mamma Mia in Summertown (8 South Parade; tel: 01865 514 141). £–££

Brasserie Blanc
71–72 Walton Street; tel: 01865 510 999; www.brasserieblanc.com; daily noon–2.45pm and 5.30–10pm.
Part of Raymond Blanc's chain of upmarket restaurants, the Brasserie Blanc serves light but traditional French dishes in a bright and airy dining room designed by Terence Conran. Children's menus available. ££–£££

The Perch
Binsey Lane; tel: 01865 728 891; www.the-perch.co.uk; Mon–Sat noon–11pm, Sun noon–10pm.
Once known as 'The Cathedral' because the landlord served alcohol on Sundays, today the pub offers an unusually extensive wine list. The restaurant serves British produce cooked with a French twist as well as a special children's menu. In summer, there is even a BBQ in the garden. £££

The Trout
195 Godstow Road, Wolvercote; tel: 01865 510 930; www.thetrout oxford.co.uk; daily 11am–11pm.
This large and comfortable riverside pub was a favourite haunt of Inspector Morse. He no doubt enjoyed the beer, but the jury's out on whether he preferred the traditional British dishes or the stone-baked pizzas. ££–£££

Above: The Trout pub boasts a stunning riverside setting.

Tour 11

Excursion to Boars Hill

About six miles (9.6 km) southwest of Oxford is Boars Hill, once famed for its panoramic view of the spires of Oxford, but now notable as a retreat from the hectic city centre

The suburbs of Oxford spread out over a wide area since the city has expanded in ribbon fashion along the main communications arteries, north, south, east and west. To the south of Oxford, beyond the ring road, large houses line the complex narrow lanes that lead to Boars Hill, an historic hamlet that offers welcome respite from the tourist crowds. The hill was long renowned for its fine views – such was the pressure of development that the Oxford Preservation Trust purchased the remaining land in 1928 to ensure that the views would not be destroyed. Despite the Trust's efforts, however, many of the original views of the city are now obscured by new development, although glimpses of the dreaming spires can

still be caught as you head uphill. But Boars Hill remains a pleasant destination in its own right, and its traditional country pubs and hotels reward the effort of the hike there.

GETTING THERE

The simplest way to travel to **Boars Hill ❶** is by bus. The No. 44 bus route (Heydordian) takes you from St Aldate's in Oxford city centre all the way there. Of course, if you are feeling energetic, you could also comfortably walk or cycle there and back in a day. Just continue down St Aldate's and on to its extension – the Abingdon Road (A4144) – until you find the turning on your right for Lake Street. At the bottom of this road, you will find a path that takes you west to the village of South Hinksey. On the far side of the village, more footpaths then take you cross-country to Boars Hill. A detailed walking map might come in handy.

Left: view of Oxford from Boars Hill.
Above: friendly encounter on the way.

JARN MOUND

Traditionally, the best place to enjoy the views at Boars Hill was the top of **Jarn Mound**, which rises up 50ft (15m) with a summit 530ft (162m) above sea level. However, new development in the city and mature trees (when in leaf) mean that the views are not what they once were. The artificial mound is of historical note, though – its construction was undertaken by the Oxford Preservation Trust and a Boars Hill resident, Sir Arthur Evans – famous for his archaeological discoveries at Knossos in Crete.

The intention was partly to provide work for the local unemployed during a period of economic depression, and partly to create a vantage point from where to admire Oxford's series of dreaming spires. It was completed in 1931 and the surrounding area planted with trees to create a wild garden. Unfortunately, it is now overgrown with bracken and scrub, and the topograph on the summit has gone, the column on which it stood broken. At various stages on the way up, however, there are good views of the city's spires. And if you go at dusk, the setting sun adds its own rich colouring to the scene. Turn round and you see another extensive view, stretching southwest over the Vale of the White Horse to the Berkshire Downs.

E Eating Out

Fox Inn
Fox Lane, Boars Hill; tel: 01865 989 221; daily noon–11pm.
This rambling timber-beamed inn on the edge of the Boars Hill village offers a traditional English pub atmosphere, with a roaring fire, regulars at the bar and a lived-in appearance. The food is standard pub fare and there is a beer garden for the summer months. £–££
Westwood Country Hotel
Hinksey Hill, near Boars Hill; tel: 01865 735 408; www.westwood hotel.co.uk; Mon–Thurs 6.30–9.30pm. The Oaks Restaurant located within this peaceful hotel set in beautiful grounds serves competently executed modern European dishes. ££–£££

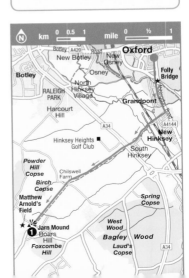

Tour 12

Excursion to Woodstock

This full day's excursion takes in the pretty Cotswold town of Woodstock as well as one of Britain's very grandest stately homes, Blenheim Palace

Situated on the A44 eight miles (13km) northwest of Oxford, Woodstock is a small English country town with an attractive main street (Park Street) flanked by fine Georgian-fronted houses and a collection of pubs, cafés and boutiques. The simplest way to get there is to take the S3 bus (Stagecoach) from Gloucester Green Bus Station in central Oxford. Buses leave every half hour, seven days a week. Once there, this tour should take you a little over a mile (2km).

TOWN HISTORY

Woodstock has a colourful history, and there was a royal manor here as far back as records go, frequented by a succession of monarchs for deer hunting when the land was still part of the great forest of Wychwood. The place name actually means 'the place in the woods', though visitors might be lulled into thinking that it derives from the five-holed wooden stocks on view outside the Oxfordshire Museum in Park Street.

Henry II installed his mistress, 'Fair' Rosamund Clifford, at Woodstock, until, so the legend goes, Queen Eleanor discovered her hunting lodge

Left: monumental Blenheim Palace.
Above: the Marlborough coat of arms
at the entrance gates of the palace.

ture and domestic life, complete with hands-on and interactive features for children. There are also temporary exhibitions, and at the back is a pleasant garden with exhibitions of contemporary sculpture.

Opposite the museum, the **Church of St Mary Magdalene** was lavishly restored in 1878, but the best part is the 18th-century tower, carved with swags of flowers around the clock and parapet.

BLENHEIM PALACE

Delightful though it is, Woodstock is somewhat overshadowed by its neighbour, the enormous **Blenheim Palace ❶** (tel: 01993 810 500; www. blenheimpalace.com; house & gardens: mid-Feb–Oct daily, Nov–mid-Dec Wed–Sun, 10.30am–5.30pm; park, all year daily, 9am–6pm or dusk; charge). Reached either on foot through the archway at the end of Park Street, or by car through the gates at the entrance to the town, this giant among English country houses lies at the heart of a vast estate covering no less than 2,700 acres (1,100 hectares).

It was built at the behest of Queen Anne for John Churchill, First Duke of Marlborough and forefather of Winston Churchill, in recognition of his

hideaway and had her murdered *(see p.106)*. Edward, the Black Prince, hero of the Hundred Years' War, was born here in 1330. And in 1554, the future Elizabeth I was imprisoned in the manor by her elder sister, Mary Tudor, for refusing to embrace Catholicism as the one true faith.

Woodstock derived much of its former prosperity, however, from glove-making. While all the factories in Woodstock itself are now closed, gloves are still made in surrounding villages and sold at the Woodstock Glove Shop to the side of the Town Hall.

OXFORDSHIRE MUSEUM

The **Oxfordshire Museum** (tel: 01993 811 456; www.tomocc.org. uk; Tue–Sat 10am–5pm, Sun 2–5pm; free) is housed in Fletcher's House on Park Street, and is well worth a visit, providing a fascinating overview of the history of Oxfordshire from the earliest times to the present day. The museum includes galleries for the displays on archaeology, agricul-

Ⓕ Sir Winston Churchill

Churchill was born on 30 November 1874 in a simple room to the west of Blenheim's Great Hall. Once used by the First Duke's domestic chaplain, Dean Jones, the room now displays many of Sir Winston's personal belongings. It was at Blenheim that Churchill proposed to his future wife, Clementine, in the Temple of Diana. The house also acted as inspiration for several of his paintings, some now on show.

great victory over the French at the Battle of Blenheim in 1704. It occupies the site of Woodstock's old Royal Manor, demolished after the Civil War. Designed by Sir John Vanbrugh and his assistant Nicholas Hawksmoor, Blenheim is recognised as a masterpiece of the English Baroque style, although its ostentatious features, and almost ruthless imposition on the English landscape, made it the subject of controversy from the moment it was completed.

Blenheim excites the imagination and invites superlatives. The skyline, with its bizarre chimneys, its pinnacles resembling stacks of cannon balls, and its ducal coronets, creates a wonderful silhouette when viewed across the lakes and avenues of the park, which was landscaped by 'Capability' Brown.

State Rooms

The attractions of the interior include the magnificent gilded **State Rooms** – adorned with an impressive array of tapestries, paintings, sculpture and fine furniture – and the beautiful **Long Library**, which contains some 10,000 volumes as well as a Willis organ. It is easy to forget, considering the scale of the palace, that it was actually built as a home. Sir Winston Churchill was born here in 1874 (see box left), and his room provides the core of an **exhibition of Churchilliana**, including manuscripts, paintings, books, photographs and letters. Unlike the First Duke of Marlborough, who is commemorated by a large monument in the palace chapel, Sir Winston is buried in a simple grave in the parish church of Bladon, on the southern periphery of the estate.

Above: the palace is surrounded by acres of superbly landscaped grounds.

Travel Tips

Active Pursuits

A visit to Oxford is not all about colleges and museums; there's also cycling, golf, ice skating, even hot-air ballooning — and plenty more for kids too. The City of Oxford is well served by sports facilities and opportunities for all kinds of active pursuits. And of course, with the river and the rolling countryside on its doorstep, there is little excuse not to get out and about.

SPORTS AND ACTIVITIES

Boating and punting

The city's rivers and canals offer the chance to try punting, rowing and canoeing, as well as to take cruises. See pages 44–45 on Oxford's waterways.

There is also, of course, the option of exploring these waterways from dry land:

Oxford Water Walks

12 Hythe Bridge Arm, Oxford Canal, Oxford; tel: 01865 798 254; www. oxfordwaterwalks.co.uk

Group walks along the towpaths of Oxford's waterways, guided by local historian and narrow-boat resident, Mark Davies. Tours provide an insight into the history and literature of the non-university side of the city.

Bowling

Bowlplex

Ozone Leisure & Entertainment Park, Grenoble Road, (bus Nos 5, 5A, 5B, 5C, 106); tel: 01865 714 100; www. bowlplexuk.com

Has 24 lanes, pool tables, video games, a fast-food restaurant and a late licence. Open 11am–10.30pm on weekdays and Sun and till midnight on Fri–Sat.

Cycling

For bicycle rental, see page 123.

Capital Sport cycling tours

The Red House, Aston Clinton, Buckinghamshire; tel: 01296 631 671; www.capital-sport.co.uk/gentle-cycling

Outdoor attractions

Many visitors to Blenheim, however, never actually go inside the palace, preferring instead to explore the attractions of its enormous park. This includes as its centrepiece **Blenheim Lake**, which is spanned by **Vanbrugh's Grand Bridge**. The shallow side, known as the Queen Pool, is well worth strolling around; home to a large variety of water fowl, it is a popular place for birdwatchers. Visitors can also hire rowing boats, and coarse fishing is possible (except mid-March to mid-June).

A further outdoor attraction is the **Marlborough Maze**, the world's largest symbolic hedge maze and an absolute must for visitors. It occupies the Walled Garden at the southern side of the estate, together with putting greens, games of giant chess and draughts, and bouncy castles. This forms part of the **Pleasure Gardens complex**, which also includes a herb and lavender garden, butterfly house, cafeteria and adventure play area.

Above: the imposing entrance.

A **miniature railway** trundles across the parkland between the palace and the pleasure gardens. The alternative is to walk, admiring on the way the magnificent gnarled oak trees, many of which bear an almost uncanny resemblance to the 'Ents' in Tolkien's *The Lord of the Rings*.

Eating Out

The Bear Hotel
Park Street, Woodstock; tel: 0844 879 9143; www.macdonaldhotels.co.uk; daily breakfast, lunch and dinner.
This romantic 13th-century coaching inn, part of the high-class Macdonald stable of hotels, has an excellent restaurant that serves modern European cooking using the highest quality organic produce. There is also the relaxing Churchill Lounge for snacks and coffee. £££

The Feathers
Market Street, Woodstock; tel: 01993 812 291; www.feathers.co.uk; daily lunch and dinner.
The Feathers hotel has won awards for its food, which is modern European in style and cooked with flair. Sunday lunch in the 17th-century

panelled dining room is a grand affair, though there is also a more informal bistro for lighter meals. £££

The Water Terrace Café
Blenheim Palace; tel: 01993 810 519; daily 10am–5.30pm.
This self-service café within the Palace offers light lunches, snacks and afternoon teas. Sit inside or out and enjoy the view over the Water Terraces. £

The Woodstock Arms
8 Market Street, Woodstock; tel: 01993 811 251; www.woodstockarms. co.uk; daily noon–11pm, food served until 9pm, Sun noon–5pm.
Old-fashioned pub in the middle of town serving comforting traditional dishes such as sausage and mash and sticky toffee pudding. Outdoor seating in the summer. ££

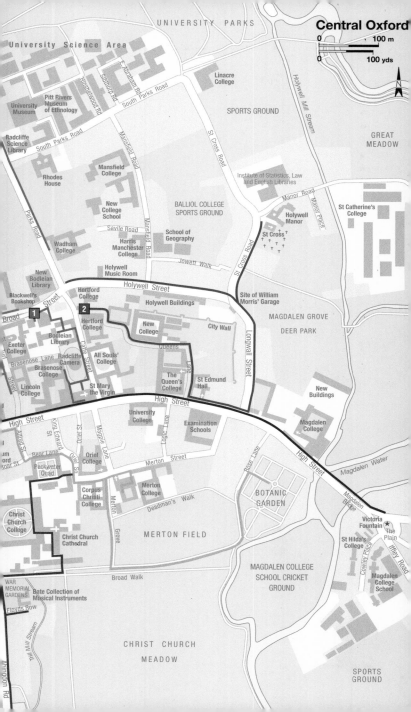

Preceding Pages: 'Blue Button' guides are noted for their expertise.
Left: try a narrow boat cruise.
Above: Oxford is very cycle friendly.

F Go-Karting

Children and adults alike will enjoy buzzing round the race track at Karting Oxford. Located just to the south of the city just off the B480 Watlington Road near to the BMW Mini car-factory (Oxford Stadium, Sandy Lane, Cowley; tel: 01865 717 134; www.kartingoxford.co.uk). Children's only sessions are held on Mondays, and restrictions apply at other times (check the website for more information).

Guided cycle rides of Oxford and the surrounding countryside take place every Saturday morning from May and throughout the summer. Tours are suitable for anyone (including children) and cycle hire is included in the (very reasonable) price. Tours leave at 10am and last around 3 hours. You need to book a place by 5pm on Wednesday, by phone, email or via the website.

Golf
Burford Golf Club
Swindon Road, Burford (19 miles/ 30km from Oxford, 1 mile off the A361); tel: 01993 822 583; www. burfordgolfclub.co.uk
A fine course, developed in the 1930s.
Frilford Heath Golf Club
Frilford Heath, near Abingdon (7 miles/ 11km from Oxford on the A338); tel: 01865 390 864; www.frilfordheath. co.uk
Three full-length golf courses.
Hinksey Heights Golf Club
South Hinksey (just off the A34 southwest of Oxford); tel: 01865 327 775; www.oxford-golf.co.uk

Relatively new course to the west of the city with stunning views of Oxford's spires. Membership or pay as you play. Lessons available. Also nature park and trail and licensed bar.
North Oxford Golf Club
Banbury Road, Oxford; tel: 01865 554 924; www.nogc.co.uk
A short course only three miles from the city centre.
Oxford Golf Club
Hill Top Road, Oxford; tel: 01865 242 158; www.oxfordgolfclub.net
Beautiful course within the ring road to the southeast of the centre, with views back to the spires of Oxford.

Above: there are plenty of golf courses in the Oxford vicinity.

Hot-air ballooning
Oxford Balloon Company
97 Whitecross, Wootton Abingdon; tel: 01235 537 429; www.oxford balloon.com
Morning and evening flights in summer offer an extraordinary opportunity to see Oxford and the surrounding countryside from a different angle.

Ice skating
Oxford Ice Rink
Oxpens Road; tel: 0844 893 3222; www.fusion-lifestyle.com
Located not far from the railway station, this ice-skating centre offers a 185 by 52ft (56 by 16m) rink, a fully licensed bar and fast food cafeteria, professional instructors, ice shows and special events, and a fully stocked skate shop.

Swimming
Hinksey Open-Air Pools
Lake Street or Abingdon Road; tel: 0844 893 3222; www.fusion-lifestyle. com. Open from the end of May until early September.

The following leisure centres have indoor pools.
Blackbird Leys Leisure Centre; Blackbird Leys; tel: 0844 893 3222; www.fusion-lifestyle.com
Ferry Sports Centre; Diamond Place, Summertown; tel: 0844 893 3222; www.fusion-lifestyle.com
Peers Sports Centre; Sandy Lane West, Littlemore; tel: 01865 467 095
Temple Cowley Pools; Temple Road, Cowley; tel: 0844 893 3222; www.fusion-lifestyle.com

Walking
Besides the walking tours available through the Oxford Information Centre on Broad Street (see p.124), more serious walkers may like to follow the Thames Path National Trail, which passes through Oxford. This is part of the National Trail Network (www.nationaltrail.co.uk; tel: 01865 810 224 for information and advice)

Above: the Didcot Railway Centre organises themed events throughout the year.

Above: there are many ways to make Oxford fun for kids.

and follows the river for 184 miles (294km) as it flows from its source in the Cotswolds to the heart of London.

CHILDREN'S ACTIVITIES

Cogges Manor Farm Museum
Church Lane, Witney; tel: 01993 772 602; www.cogges.org; Tue–Sun 10am–5pm; charge.

Little ones will be captivated by the hand milking and butter-making, as well as crafts demonstrations that are held in the barn.

Didcot Railway Centre
Didcot; tel: 01235 817 200; www. didcotrailwaycentre.org.uk; Sat–Sun 10.30am–4.30pm, consult website for other days of opening; charge.

Young steam buffs should be taken to the Didcot Railway Centre, though make sure to telephone beforehand to enquire when the steam trains will be put through their paces.

Science Oxford
1–5 London Place; tel: 01865 728 953; www.scienceoxford.com; Mon–Sat 10am–5pm; charge

As well as a great number of special children's events, there is a permanent exhibition and a 'discovery zone' for younger kids.

Shotover Country Park
Old Road, Headington; tel: 01865 249 811; www.oxford.gov.uk/leisure; daily; free

This is a delight for all those who like playing hide and seek and climbing trees; there is also a 'natural' sandpit for the younger ones.

Animals and Railways

Cutteslowe Park (Harbord Road; daily; free) to the north of the city centre has an aviary as well as a miniature train circuit (also playgrounds and mini-golf). Cotswold Wildlife Park, a half-hour drive from the city near the attractive town of Burford (tel: 01993 823 006; www.cotswoldwildlifepark.co.uk; daily 10am–6pm or dusk if earlier; charge) has even greater delights, with rhinos, monkeys and crocodiles as well as – again – a narrow-gauge railway.

Above: swans on the pond at Cutteslowe Park.

Themed Holidays

Holidays in and around Oxford need not be a standard whistle-stop tour around sights and museums. Oxfordshire's natural assets lend themselves to a variety of activities.

Cultural vacations

Oxford University's Department of Continuing Education (tel: 01865 270 360; www.conted.ox.ac.uk) run summer courses – some residential – and programmes of lectures in a wide variety of subjects including creative writing, history of art, and philosophy.

ACE Study Tours (tel: 01223 835 055; www.acestudytours.co.uk) run high-quality cultural holidays in Oxford and other places. They will also tailor-make a tour to suit your needs.

Horse riding

Valley Farm Equestrian Centre
Mollington Lane, Shotteswell, Banbury; tel: 01295 730 576; www.valleyfarmequestriancentre.co.uk
With B.H.S.-qualified instructors, this school has something for riders of all ages and abilities. As well as day courses and a summer camp, there is the chance of hacking in beautiful countryside.

Standlake Equestrian Centre and Ranch
Downs Road, Standlake, Witney; tel: 01865 300 099; www.standlakeranch.co.uk
As well as tuition and other activities, this centre offers residential 'Ranch Riding' holidays and family ranch holidays in self-catering chalets.

Narrow boats

A holiday aboard a narrow boat will give you a taste for the sort of simple life evoked in Kenneth Grahame's *The Wind in the Willows* (which was inspired by the Oxfordshire countryside).

College Cruisers Narrow boats
Combe Road Wharf, Oxford; tel: 01865 554 343; www.collegecruisers.com
Offers 2- to 12-berth canal boats for short breaks or longer holidays.

Oxfordshire Narrow boats
Canal Wharf, Station Road, Lower Heyford, Bicester; tel: 01869 340 348; www.oxfordshire-narrowboats.co.uk
A 200-year-old working boatyard with a fleet of holiday narrow boats for hire.

Walking and nature holidays

Headwater (tel: 01606 720 199; www.headwater.com) organise walking and cycling holidays with accommodation and other arrangements all made for you. Their walk from Stratford to Oxford is especially popular.

Footpath Holidays (tel: 01985 840 049; www.footpath-holidays.com) run a variety of walking vacations, and will also tailor a trip along a particular theme (eg literary, historical), according to your requirements.

Above: the Oxford Canal at Jericho.

Practical Information

All the essential practical information you need to make your trip to Oxford run smoothly.

GETTING THERE

By plane
Flights from both Europe and the US arrive at London's two major airports, Heathrow (tel: 0844 335 1801; www.heathrowairport.com) and Gatwick (tel: 0844 892 0322; www.gatwickairport.com), as well as at London City Airport (tel: 020 7646 0088; www.londoncityairport.com) and Birmingham International Airport (tel: 0871 222 0072; www.birminghamairport.co.uk). Flights from European destinations also arrive at London Stansted (tel: 0844 335 1803; www.stanstedairport.com) and London Luton Airport (tel: 01582 405 100; www.london-luton.co.uk).

From Heathrow, the Oxford Bus Company operates the Airline coach service, which departs every half hour during the daytime and roughly every hour and a half at night; the journey takes 1.5 hours. Their Airline bus to and from Gatwick runs every hour during the day, every 2 hours at night, and the journey time is around 2.5 hours. National Express (www.nationalexpress.com) run coaches between Oxford and London Stansted. There are regular train connections from Birmingham to Oxford, as well as several coach services a day operated by National Express; the latter take 1.5 hours.

By car
From London and the Midlands, Oxford is well served by the M40 motorway, which passes within 8 miles (13km) north of the city. The journey from central London takes about 1.5 hours, except during rush hour when it can take considerably longer to get out of London along the A40 Westway. Drivers coming from London should exit at Junction 8, while those coming from the Midlands should turn off at Junction 9. If you are travelling from either Gatwick or Heathrow airports, join the M40 via the London orbital motorway, the M25. From the Cotswolds, take the A40 or A44 to Oxford.

By bus
Services from London to Oxford's Gloucester Green Bus Station are good value and extremely regular. The Oxford Tube (tel: 01865 772 250; www.oxfordtube.com) departs from London about every 15 minutes during the daytime and at 20-minute intervals for most of the evening from Grosvenor Gardens (near Victoria Railway Station). This bus also stops en route at Marble Arch, Notting Hill Gate and Shepherd's Bush. Oxford Espress X90 coaches, operated by the Oxford Bus Company (tel: 01865 785 400; www.oxfordbus.co.uk), leave London's Victoria Coach Station every 15 or 20 minutes (15–30 minutes at weekends),

Above: the reliable Oxford Tube.

and also stop at Marble Arch and Baker Street on the way. Most journeys take about 1 hour 40 minutes, but during rush-hour you should allow for likely traffic congestion in London.

By train
There are frequent trains between London Paddington and Oxford, departing roughly every half an hour. For timetable information contact the National Rail Enquiry Service (tel: 08457 48 49 50; www.nationalrail.co.uk).

Parking
Parking in central Oxford is very limited, and in residential areas you often need a resident's parking permit. There are large car parks at Hythe Bridge Street, Gloucester Green and St Clements (all pay and display) as well as a multi-storey car park behind the Westgate Shopping Centre. Further pay and display parking is available either side of St Giles', but during the day it is difficult to find a place.

Visitors should note that traffic wardens in Oxford are extremely vigilant (and work on commission).

GETTING AROUND
Public transport
Within central Oxford, the Oxford Bus Company (tel: 01865 785 400; www.oxfordbus.co.uk) and Stagecoach (tel: 01865 772 250; www.stagecoachbus.com) operate bus services. Both companies offer special day-return tickets, family tickets, as well as travel cards with unlimited travel in the city. All tickets are purchased from the driver. Regional Bus Services, including those to Woodstock for Blenheim Palace, operate from Gloucester Green Coach Station.

By car
Hire cars
Avis, 1 Abbey Road; tel: 0844 544 6087; www.avis.co.uk
Budget, Unit 1, Oxford Business Centre, Osney Lane; tel: 01865 724 884; www.budget.co.uk

Above: it may be hard to park your car in town, but not your bike.

Enterprise, 53 West Way, Botley; tel: 01865 202 088; www.enterprise.co.uk
Europcar, Littlemead Business Park, Ferry Hinksey Road; tel: 01865 246 373; www.europcar.co.uk

Bike rental

Cycling is popular in Oxford and, as well as many cycleways, there are clear signs to enable cyclists to avoid the main thoroughfares. Bicycles can be hired from Bainton Bikes (Walton Street Cycles, 78 Walton Street and Train Station; tel: 01865 311 610; www.baintonbikes.com); Bike Zone (St Michael Street; tel: 01865 728 877; www.bike-zone.co.uk) and Summertown Cycles (202 Banbury Road; tel: 01865 316 885; www.summertowncycles.co.uk).

Taxis

Taxi ranks are found at St Aldate's, St Giles, Gloucester Green and at the railway station. Because of Oxford's one-way system, metered fares can be high.
ABC Taxis, tel: 01865 775 577.
001 Taxis; tel: 01865 240 000; www.001taxis.com.
Radio Taxis, tel: 01865 242 424.

GOING GREEN

Oxford scores relatively well on going green, with its pedestrianised central zones, Park and Ride scheme, low-emission buses and multitude of cyclists. Green initiatives pushed through by the City Council in recent years include helping the university to switch to green electricity, achieving 100 percent door-to-door recycling in the city, supporting measures such as reusable nappy schemes, offering home-insulation grants, introducing hundreds of new bike racks in the city and planting trees across Oxford. For energy advice and information on recycling facilities in the city, see www.oxford.gov.uk/environment/index.cfm; see also www.oxfordismyworld.org for information on how to reduce your carbon footprint.

FACTS FOR THE VISITOR

Disabled travellers

For details of premises that are accessible to wheelchairs, call the Access Officer at Oxford City Council on tel: 01865 249 811 or visit www.oxford.gov.uk. Free wheelchairs or scooters can be borrowed from Oxford Shopmobility (booking tel: 01865 248737), a scheme funded by the City Council.

Emergencies

Police, ambulance, fire brigade, tel: 999. Thames Valley Police, St Aldate's, non-emergency tel: 101.
John Radcliffe Hospital (with accident and emergency unit), Headley Way, Headington, tel: 01865 741 166; www.oxfordradcliffe.nhs.uk
NHS Direct (helpline): 0845 4647.

Opening hours

Most of the city-centre shops open Monday to Saturday 9am–5.30pm; many also open on Sunday from 10am–4pm. There is late-night shopping (until around 8.30pm) on Thursday. Most businesses operate from 9am to 5.30pm, Monday to Friday.

> **F Park and Ride**
>
> If you want to avoid the problem of parking, use the Park and Ride service. You can park your car and then take the bus into central Oxford from the Pear Tree or Water Eaton car parks in the north (A34, A44, or A4260); the Redbridge car park in the south (A34 or A4074); Seacourt in the west (A40 or A420); and Thornhill in the east (A40 from London). All operate daily, except Seacourt, which is closed on Sundays.

Tourist information

The Oxford Information Centre at
15–16 Broad Street (tel: 01865 252
200; www.visitoxfordandoxfordshire.
com) has a wealth of information on
the city, including a selection of maps
and guides. The centre also helps with
accommodation and organises guided
tours. Open Mon–Sat 9.30am–5pm,
Sun and bank holidays 10am–3pm.

ENTERTAINMENT

For details on concert venues and theatres, see pages 24–25.

Cinema

The city has two Odeons (George
Street and Magdalen Street; tel:
0871 224 4007; www.odeon.co.uk)
plus the independent Phoenix Pic-
turehouse (57 Walton Street; tel:
0871 902 5736; www.picturehouses.
co.uk) and the Ultimate Picture Palace (Jeune Street; tel: 01865 245
288; www.uppcinema.co.uk).

Nightlife

Oxford's premier nightclub is Lava and
Ignite (Park End Street; tel: 01865 250
181) with three dance floors. Others
include The Bridge (6–9 Hythe Bridge
Street; tel: 01865 242 526; www.bridge
oxford.co.uk); Escape (9a High Street;
tel: 01865 246 766; www.escape-
oxford.co.uk), Lola Lo Tiki Bar & Club
(13–15 Magdalen Street; tel: 01865 249
171; www.lolalooxford.com) and Rop-
pongi (29–31 George Street; tel: 01865
242 200; www.roppongioxford.co.uk).

For comedy, there is a branch of The
Glee Club (3 Hythe Bridge Street; tel:
0871 472 0400; www.glee.co.uk). Jericho is a good area for bars, including the
long-established Duke of Cambridge
(5–6 Little Clarendon Street; tel: 01865
558173, www.dukebar.com); trendy
Raoul's (32 Walton Street; tel: 01865
553 732, www.raoulsbar.co.uk) and
Freud (see p.95). Also try the Cowley
Road, where the Kazbar (25–27 Cowley Road; tel: 01865 202 920, www.kaz
bar.co.uk) serves cocktails and tapas in
a Moroccan-inspired setting.

Above: there is a vibrant theatre scene in Oxford (see p.24–25).

Accommodation

Make your Oxford stay special by choosing a classic historic hotel, a traditional B&B or even the city's former prison.

Accommodation in Oxford is not cheap, and while there are plenty of bed and breakfasts, there is only a very limited number of hotels. Booking ahead is therefore essential, especially in summer. For visitors arriving without accommodation, the Oxford Information Centre on Broad Street offers a room booking service for a small fee. During the university vacations you may be able to stay in college rooms, through the University Rooms scheme (www.oxfordrooms.co.uk).

Price ranges for a hotel room for one night for a double room (quoted as a guide only) are as follows:

£££	over £150
££	£75–150
£	under £75

OXFORD CITY

Bath Place Hotel
4–5 Bath Place; tel: 01865 791 812; www.bathplace.co.uk.
A charming family-run hotel occupying a group of restored 17th-century cottages in the heart of Oxford right next door to the Turf Tavern. Reputedly the scene of Richard Burton–Elizabeth Taylor trysts. ££

Burlington House
374 Banbury Road; tel: 01865 513 513; www.burlington-hotel-oxford.co.uk.
A stylishly decorated and furnished hotel in a lovely Victorian property within easy walking distance of the Summertown shopping parade in North Oxford. Has 12 spacious bedrooms, excellent service and great breakfast. ££

Cotswold Lodge Hotel
66a Banbury Road; tel: 01865 512 121; www.cotswoldlodgehotel.co.uk.

Four-star hotel set in a beautiful Victorian building just outside the city centre. The rooms – some inspired by and named after colleges – are traditional in style and very comfortable. Facilities include a bar and restaurant. ££

Macdonald Randolph Hotel
Beaumont Street; tel: 0844 879 9132; www.macdonaldhotels.co.uk.
A city landmark, located opposite the Ashmolean Museum, and Oxford's most famous hotel. Grand tradition rules, from the decor in the rooms to the classic afternoon tea in the drawing room (a favourite for post-graduation celebrations) to the wood-panelled Morse Bar. £££

Malmaison
3 Oxford Castle; tel: 01865 268 400; www.malmaison.com/Oxford.
Occupying the former prison – with each room consisting of three cells

Above: the Malmaison Hotel, set in an old prison at Oxford Castle.

knocked into one – this stylish boutique hotel offers the ultimate escape. Rooms offer internet access, DVD players and roll-top baths. Elsewhere in the hotel is a chic brasserie and bar, and a gym. £££

Mercure Eastgate Hotel

73 High Street; tel: 01865 791 681; www.accorhotels.com.

A former 17th-century coaching inn, the traditional-style Eastgate is located adjacent to the site of Oxford's old East Gate and opposite the Examination Schools. Facilities include a restaurant and bar. ££

Old Bank Hotel

92–94 High Street; tel: 01865 799 599; www.oldbank-hotel.co.uk.

One of the city's most stylish hotels, housed in an elegant Georgian former bank. Rooms are contemporary in style. The fashionable Quod Brasserie is downstairs. £££

Old Parsonage Hotel

1 Banbury Road; tel: 01865 310 210; www.oldparsonage-hotel.co.uk.

An upmarket, well-located hotel in the renovated old parsonage next to St Giles' church. Luxuriously appointed en-suite bedrooms with stylish decor. The excellent hotel restaurant is open to non-residents and also offers excellent afternoon tea. £££

The Tower House

15 Ship Street; tel: 0871 376 9900; www.oxfordhotelsandinns.com.

Located centrally off Cornmarket, this friendly, family-run guesthouse dates to the 17th century. The seven bedrooms are furnished with antiques and decorated to a high standard. £–££

OUTSIDE OXFORD

The Feathers

Market Street, Woodstock; tel: 01993 812 291; www.feathers.co.uk.

This 17th-century hotel in the centre of this market town near Blenheim Palace has 20 cosy traditionally furnished rooms, one with its own steam room. The hotel restaurant is celebrated for its fine modern English food. £££

Le Manoir aux Quat'Saisons

Church Road, Great Milton; tel: 01844 278 881; www.manoir.com.

Raymond Blanc's glorious manor house offers the ultimate gastronomic hotel experience, with elegantly decorated traditional-style bedrooms, beauty therapies and, of course, his two Michelin-starred restaurant. £££

Otmoor Lodge

Horton Hill, Horton-Cum-Studley; tel: 01865 351 235; www.otmoor lodge.co.uk.

This 18th-century inn with modern rooms offers peace and tranquillity on Oxford's doorstep. The upmarket restaurant serves tasty dishes. ££

Weston Manor

Northampton Road, Weston on the Green; tel: 01869 350 621; www. westonmanor.co.uk.

This impressive 17th-century manor house is set in 12 acres (5 hectares) of beautiful gardens and has a croquet lawn and outdoor heated pool. Excellent cuisine is served in the Baronial Hall and there is also a cosy lounge for afternoon tea. £££

WEBSITES

Guest houses/B&Bs: www.oxford city.co.uk (for B&Bs, guest houses, camping, hostels, pubs, inns, etc); www. bnbselect.com; www.bedandbreak fasts-uk.co.uk; www.visitengland.com (accommodation across England); www.visitoxfordandoxfordshire.com (Oxford Information Centre site – helps with accommodation booking)

Boutique hotels: www.mrandmrs smith.com; www.tablethotels.com

Green: www.greentraveller.co.uk; www.responsibletravel.com

Self-catering: www.oxstay.co.uk; www.nationaltrustcottages.co.uk; www.landmarktrust.org.uk

Index

Credits

Insight Great Breaks Oxford
Written by: Tony Halliday, Michael Macaroon
Edited by: Tom Stainer
Art Editor: Richard Cooke
Maps: APA Publications
Publishing Manager: Rachel Fox
Series Editor: Sarah Clark

Photography by: Alamy 30T, 118, 119B; AKG London 89T; Andrew Gray 82T, 108T; Art Archive 88B/T; Blenheim Palace and Jarrolds Publishing 110; CHK 111, 113; Fotolia 20B, 26B, 64B, 70/71; Christian Guthier 101B; Corrie Wingate/ Apa Publications 15, 21B/T, 46T, 102T, 119T; Garrettc 74B; APA Glyn Genin 9T, 32B/T, 33T, 42B, 44/45, 44B/M/T, 48, 49B, 63T, 70B, 73T, 90B, 91B, 93B, 94T, 99B, 101T, 102B, 103T, 106, 107T, 112B, 114/115, 120; Dreamstime 2/3, 14, 18, 87, 120; Grue 42T; Getty 37, 52; iStockphoto, 4BR, 4TL, 5CR, 6/7, 7B, 8T, 17B/T, 18/19, 19B, 26T, 29B, 30B, 49T, 50B, 37B, 38B/T, 41, 62T, 69T, 74T, 87T, 96T, 98B, 122B; Jerome Bump 4BL, 5BR/TR, 50T, 51B; Frank Noon/Apa Publications 2/3T, 8, 10; Kobal 84/85, 84T; Leonardo 23B; Lincoln Library 39T; Malmaison Oxford 83B, Mary Evans 84C; 125; Museum of Modern Art 66B, 66T, 68; National Portrait gallery 35MR; O'Massey 93T; Oxford-University Press Museum 92B/T; 117T Photolibrary; Pictures Colour Library 5BL, 121; Photoshot 24/25; Rex Features 34T, 84B; Sheldinian Theatre 16; Spoonerisms 28B; Kaihushu Tai 106T; Tony Halliday/Apa Publications 5TR, 28/29, 31T, 35TL, 40B/T, 60B, 61B, 72B, 89B, 97T, 104T, 105T; Topfoto 24TL, 124; University Museum 5CL; University of Oxford Botanic Gardens 52B, 99T, 100T; Urban legend 47; Cover pictures by: 4Corners Images (T) and iStockphoto (BR) Frank Noon /Apa Publications (BL).

CONTACTING THE EDITORS: As every effort is made to provide accurate information in this publication, we would appreciate it if readers would call our attention to any errors and omissions by contacting: Apa Publications, PO Box 7910, London SE1 1WE, England. Fax: (44 20) 7403 0290. E-mail: insight@apaguide.co.uk

Information has been obtained from sources believed to be reliable, but its accuracy and completeness, and the opinions based thereon, are not guaranteed.

© 2014 APA Publications (UK) Ltd.
Second Edition 2014
Printed in China by CTPS

Worldwide distribution enquiries:
APA Publications GmbH & Co. Verlag KG (Singapore Branch), 7030 Ang Mo Kio Ave 5 08-65 Northstar @ AMK Singapore 569880 apasin@singnet.com.sg
Distributed in the UK and Ireland by:
Dorling Kindersley Ltd (a Penguin Company) 80 Strand, London WC2R 0RL, UK sales@uk.dk.com
Distributed in the United States by:
Ingram Publisher Services 1 Ingram Boulevard, PO Box 3006, La Vergne, TN 37086-1986 ips@ingramcontent.com